The Kindred Life

The Kindred Life

STORIES & RECIPES TO CULTIVATE A
LIFE OF ORGANIC CONNECTION

CHRISTINE MARIE BAILEY

HARPER HORIZON

Published by Harper Horizon, an imprint of HarperCollins Focus LLC.

Published in association with literary agent Jenni Burke of Illuminate Literary Agency, www.illluminateliterary.com.

Unless otherwise noted below, photos are courtesy of the author's personal archives.

The photos on the following pages are copyright © Sarah B. Gilliam: 12, 22, 54, 66, 80, 100, 103, 105, 120–21, 162, 186, 188–89, 192, 204, 210, 220, 222, 224, 228.

The photos on the following pages are copyright © Jeremy Cowart: 134–35, 202, 230.

Any internet addresses, phone numbers, or company or product information printed in this book are offered as a resource and are not intended in any way to be or to imply an endorsement by Harper Horizon, nor does Harper Horizon vouch for the existence, content, or services of these sites, phone numbers, companies, or products beyond the life of this book.

Unless otherwise noted, Scripture quotations are taken from the Holy Bible, New Living Translation. Copyright © 1996, 2004, 2015 by Tyndale House Foundation. Used by permission of Tyndale House Publishers, Carol Stream, Illinois 60188. All rights reserved.

Scripture quotations marked TPT are taken from The Passion Translation®. Copyright © 2017, 2018 by Passion & Fire Ministries, Inc. Used by permission. All rights reserved. ThePassionTranslation.com.

This is a work of nonfiction. The events and experiences detailed herein are all true and have been faithfully rendered as remembered by the author, to the best of her ability. Some names have been changed to protect the privacy of the individuals involved.

ISBN 978-0-7852-4110-2 (eBook)
ISBN 978-0-7852-4109-6 (HC)

Library of Congress Control Number: 2021944114

Printed in South Korea
22 23 24 25 26   SAM   10 9 8 7 6 5 4 3 2 1

To Jesus, my Rescuer, Friend, Comforter, and Guide.
You have saved me,
spoken love over me,
given me a voice,
walked beside me,
fought my battles,
and wooed me with beauty,
every single day of my life.
In the end, it's you and me.

Contents

"

The world will tell you how

to live, if you let it.

Don't let it.

Take up your space.

Raise your voice.

Sing your song.

This is your chance to

make or remake a

life that thrills you.

—SHAUNA NIEQUIST,
PRESENT OVER PERFECT

CHAPTER 1

Sing Your Song

Have you ever heard a mockingbird singing in the middle of the night? One evening, tucked under my white comforter in our cozy 1940s farmhouse, I did. It stirred my husband, Steven, and me as we were drifting away in that drowsy state of almost-but-not-quite asleep.

"That's one confused mockingbird," he mumbled, while I lay there alert, in wonder. For the next thirty minutes, its solo song delightfully haunted me. During the day on our land in Tennessee, birdsong is usually accompanied by many other sounds: hums of mowers and cars whizzing down the country road at fifty miles per hour, our little girls' voices and giggles, our cat's meows, dramatic chicken cackles—all the banging and clanging of daily farm life.

As the state bird of Tennessee, mockingbirds are common here. They serenade us from the treetops above the produce field and from the barn roof apex. They dive-bomb us when we pass too closely to their nests. But a single mockingbird singing an ever-changing song in the middle of the night outside our bedroom window? This was a first. It had me pondering. Did it not know it was nighttime? Did it realize it was the only one singing? Did it even care?

We moved to our land in Tennessee in December 2016, the dead of winter. It had been a farm in World War II times, but no remnant of anything fruitful remained except for a totally endearing yet scraggly apple tree enjoyed primarily by squirrels. We settled into the restored olive-green farmhouse on seventeen acres of possibility and started drawing out plans for our dreams: to beautify the land, to make it a home for us and for animals, to grow organic food for us and the community, and to gather people around the table at farm dinners filled with abundance.

We broke ground on the first day of spring 2017, and before that, I'd never farmed a day in my life. Steven and I had dreamed of having our own farm "one day," but when it became a reality, I resisted it wholeheartedly at first, fearing the potential isolation of living in the country and not knowing if I was cut out for the taxing manual labor of birthing a farm.

Grit was practically a foreign word to me. I didn't like pushing through hard things, and my first instinct was to quit when situations got too tough, messy, or uncomfortable. Heck, I didn't even like being dirty, and I really, really liked wearing makeup.

But only three months after that groundbreaking day, I'd worn some serious creases into my leather farm boots, and my palms had not one but two rows of calluses. We'd transformed a huge open field full of three-foot-tall weeds into a lush organic garden: a half acre of every shade of green, vines heavy with cucumbers snaking the ground, armfuls of magenta radishes and crimson beets, mini forests of kale and rainbow chard. People were buying our stuff at farmers markets. The meadows where the piglets roamed were regrowing a deep emerald green.

As the land was being transformed, something inside me was healing and growing too.

You see, I've always struggled to find what's uniquely mine to offer the world.

One of the biggest misconceptions I had growing up in the church was that I had to have a certain personality to truly shine and contribute something meaningful. It seemed the boisterous, extroverted, gregarious girls were the ones who were celebrated, and there was somehow something wrong with me since I didn't want to be the center of attention. My more reserved and artistic personality, talents, and gifts seemed more hidden and less important.

So I was easily compliant, merging with others' dreams and plans in an effort to avoid conflict and struggle. All the while, desires burned within me: to point others to beauty, to gather people together in a meaningful way, to have a life infused with bravery and adventure, to appreciate the body God has given me, as imperfect as it is.

A song has been deep inside all along, waiting to be sung.

Oh, I've had plenty of chances to do things I truly love. I grew up an Italian American girl in New Jersey and ventured off on my own to Tennessee for college. In my early to mid twenties, I had a job I loved in the music industry, journeyed to India and Kenya and

Uganda, and helped start an Africa relief organization. I began blogging and freelance writing to share the words that wanted to pour out of me.

By my early thirties, I became a mother, the number one job I've always wanted. I was delightfully immersed in new motherhood, and even with a little daughter underfoot—and then a few years later, a second one—I still built in outlets for creativity, nature, adventure, and play. I was surprised by the new fierceness and boldness that surfaced when it came to protecting my family's values or my daughter's childhood. Yet I still clung to safety and predictability when I was on my own. By the time my late thirties approached, I felt a deep stirring to learn more about myself and my capabilities. What did *I* uniquely have to offer? And was there even more I could learn and experience if I opened myself up to risk and change?

Shortly after we began farming day-to-day, I was presented with a choice: continue shrinking back in fear or start showing up in courage. I dipped my pinkie toe into a new life, setting, and vocation, showing up in my vulnerable yet authentic self. And the world didn't end. It actually felt . . . *really good*.

Soon, I began to see a pattern developing:

Walk through uncertainty and discomfort with every bit of courage I can muster.
Push through challenges.
Grow.
See how much better it is on the other side.

On a farm, you don't get to choose whether or not you want to do hard things. That first farming season, I learned how to properly handle a chicken. I learned how to fix the myriad irrigation leaks. I learned how to seed a cover crop without dumping the whole bag of seeds in one spot again (oops). I learned how to podcast, speak the truth more boldly, play the ukulele, and write for my first print magazine. I accomplished these things not because of some sort of magic and not because I wasn't afraid sometimes, but because I just began. And each time, I had a little more courage to keep going.

Over the last several years, since we founded the farm, my body has been pushed to its physical limits. I've worked muscles I didn't even know existed to lift soil with the broadfork, hammer stakes, and use what's appropriately called "the farmer walk" to haul a bucket of water with each arm up a hill. I've broken down when it all seemed too much: when butternut squash was taken over by beetles, when we lost two months of lettuce seedlings to pests, and when I felt like I couldn't spend *one more single day* of summer sweating down to my underwear by 7:30 a.m.

Of all the things I thought I could possibly be, a farmer was never one of them. But to my complete and utter surprise, I've found a deep well of strength and joy while digging into the soil of Kindred Farm.

After struggling with body image for much of my life, I've learned my body is stronger than I ever thought possible. Now, even though body image is still a big challenge for me, I know I'd rather be strong than a certain size and that my beauty glows from the inside out—yes, even through a sweaty, makeup-free face that's been harvesting lettuce for hours.

Sifting soil through my hands has made my faith more real, and I feel more connected to the earth God gave me, both for its beauty and its functionality. I'm a partner in redeeming that earth, little by little, through growing food and flowers and sharing fruits of the earth with others in a way that helps us all slow down and connect.

Looking back, I can see how every step of the journey has led me to this place where I truly, finally, feel at home—welcoming people to our land and pursuing a nourishing life of connection, infused with both beauty and grit.

With all the blunders, mistakes, and learning experiences, I'm finding my voice and the song that's uniquely mine to sing.

So do you want to know what I discovered about why a mockingbird sings in the middle of the night?

In his article for the *Los Angeles Times*, biologist and science writer William Jordan shared a similar story of being awakened in the dark by a sole mockingbird singing loudly. He explained that although mockingbirds can be territorial, they don't want to fight physically because of potential injury that would cost them too much. So they rely on the "vigor and skill" of their songs.

The mockingbird I heard singing in the middle of the night was singing for his family's survival, and "singing was the measure of his substance and grit."[1]

In my mind, I had romanticized birdsong into a joyous, rainbows-and-butterflies scene from children's storybooks. But here's the truth: mockingbirds don't just sing for joy—they sing because they have to. There's both a strength and beauty to the mockingbird's gorgeous, gritty song . . . and to my song, and to your song too.

And here's the great news: a life of organic connection isn't something that only happens on a farm in Tennessee; it happens in your suburban neighborhood, your city living room. It's not about *where* you live but *how*.

Maybe you need to be nourished on a soul level because right now you feel depleted and unable to love others, or yourself, well.

Maybe you desperately want a childhood that unravels slowly for your children and a slower, less busy, less chaotic life, but you don't know how to change things.

Maybe you've buried some of your gifts and desires because of fear of what it might take to *just go for it* or because of others' expectations of what your life should look like.

Maybe you ache for a life of deep community but don't know how to find it or if it's even possible anymore.

This book is for you.

The Kindred Life is a rally cry for connection in a time when we need to recapture what's been lost in the chaos of busyness, distraction, and isolation. We find it again by investing in the things that have always mattered and fed our souls since the beginning of time: authentic connection with flesh-and-blood people, the soil beneath our feet, and life around the table.

This is a return to what is good. This is a reclaiming.

It's time to sing the song you've been given to sing. To push through challenges, start walking out dreams that have been hidden in your heart, and take steps forward in flickering moments of bravery so you can live the Kindred Life you're meant to live.

Come along on this journey with me, and you'll learn what it means to cultivate a rich, nourishing life of organic connection. Right where you are.

But first, let's go back to where it all began, on a January afternoon in the middle of a blizzard in Branson, Missouri.

THIS CHAPTER IS ABOUT

We all have a song inside that's waiting to be sung. Our voices may be gritty and imperfect at first, but it's time to start singing.

- What does bravery mean to you?

- Name a time when you felt the most "you" you've ever been. Write a few thoughts about when and where you were and how it felt.

- While reading this chapter, what inner "song" began to come to the surface? *Pay attention* to that now and make note of what you're sensing.

- What does your unique "voice" sound and look like?

- What are you proud of in yourself? What do you like about the life you're living?

- What are some things you'd like to change?

"

It turns out that playing it safe,

at least in matters of the heart, is

the most dangerous

thing you can do.

By that route, you become a butterfly pinned

to the wall, with wonderful colors and all

kinds of potential but going nowhere.

Your wings are clipped. To really fly you must

claim the courage to

live out of your real self,

the one God called you into being.

—PAULA RINEHART,
STRONG WOMEN, SOFT HEARTS

CHAPTER 2

That Guy in Dallas

I saw him walking across the exhibit hall in a T-shirt, khakis, and vintage gray New Balance sneakers. He was doing this thing with his eyes that made me notice their almond shape and his long lashes. Now, sixteen years later, I know he was just trying to read something in the distance. I recall what I was wearing too: my favorite flare-leg jeans and a long-sleeve, asymmetrical-neck black shirt. My curly hair was flat-ironed and highlighted within an inch of its life.

It was January 2004 in Branson, Missouri, and I was at the first-ever conference for the college student leaders of Kanakuk Kamps. I had been invited as a vendor because I was working with the leader of the conference to recruit street-team volunteers for Mel Gibson's controversial film, *The Passion of the Christ*.

After graduating from Belmont University in Nashville with a music business degree five years before, I had been working full-time in the Christian music industry, running the Nashville office of Grassroots Music, a promotions agency for artists like Caedmon's Call, Bebo Norman, Andrew Peterson, Third Day, and Jars of Clay and, most recently, for films. This was before the age of social media, so we relied on true "grassroots" promotion methods: phone calls, posters, message boards, and the gracious help of street-team volunteers who signed up to spread the word with their actual voices in front of actual people.

The conference needed exhibitors, and I needed to get in front of a bunch of college students, so I dragged my friends Suz and Tara-Leigh from Nashville through the winding Ozark Mountains in a snowstorm. Only one other exhibitor was there, the guy I'd seen earlier who seemed to be of East Asian descent, whose table was next to ours.

As I was setting up, he said, "Hi! I love your Mac computer," and flashed one of the biggest, brightest smiles I'd ever seen.

I turned toward him. Those eyes and that smile. *Who is this guy?*

We introduced ourselves, and I learned his name was Steven Bailey, and he was from Dallas, Texas. As we went about our morning, chatting with college students and trying to sign them up for our causes, he kept coming over to our table to strike up conversation. Suz and Tara-Leigh finally gave me The Look, pulled me aside, and told me what they'd both been thinking: "Stine, that guy has a crush on someone at this table, and it's *not* us."

I had to admit, he was magnetic from moment number one. Without even realizing it, I let the protective wall I'd built around my single life cave a tiny bit, and what began as flirty small talk about our computers quickly led to impassioned conversations where I, at age twenty-five, felt an ease I had never experienced before with a guy. The words spilled out my mouth, and I felt no need to think about what to say next.

Steven listened intently as I shared my love for a nonprofit in India called Peace Gospel International, which I'd been intimately involved with since 1999 through my friend who had started the organization. I dreamed of traveling there and meeting the native Indian director, Pastor Samuel, and his family and getting to see the projects I'd helped support firsthand. Would I be brave enough to actually take the leap?

As I shared all of this with a guy I'd just met hours before, a flickering light inside me glowed a little stronger. *Did someone out there really understand the wild dreams that had been stirring within me?*

I learned that Steven was half Korean on his mother's side, had lived in South Korea as a child, and had learned Korean as his first language. His father's side of the family descended from tobacco farmers in North Carolina. After graduating from Baylor a few years before, he'd started 963 Missions, a travel company that connected people (mainly college students) who wanted to serve with nonprofit organizations established in various countries.

He'd spent three summers holding babies at crowded orphanages in Romania and had recently traveled to Indonesia, where he was the only one in his group who didn't hesitate to eat the raw lettuce in a traditional meal served to them in a remote village, enjoying it with utter abandon and falling violently ill thirty minutes later. He loved coffee and baseball and really, *really* loved food—eating and cooking and baking. Steven was a fiery ball of enthusiasm, from his booming voice to the way he spoke animatedly with his hands to the way his freaking gorgeous eyes locked on mine.

And then he said he was planning a trip later that year to Italy, the homeland of my Sicilian immigrant grandfather and many more relatives on my dad's side. I'd traveled to Italy for the first time with my mom less than a year before, and the whole experience had been pure magic. I'm sure my face lit up when I told him about stuffing my pockets with washed-up lavender and turquoise tiles on the beaches of the Cinque Terre and drinking limoncello in the shadow of Mount Vesuvius and eating the best pizza of my life on the shores of Lake Como.

The sparks began to fly, lighting up every square inch of that chilly, drab conference hall in the middle of Branson, Missouri.

The room couldn't contain what was brewing: a deep partnership that would, a few years in the future, withstand unimaginable difficulties, weather multiple business failures, walk through broken relationships, and build and rebuild our lives multiple times. Within those four beige walls was the potential for a love that would beat hard against darkness and odds. It would be unlike the shiny stock images of couples on church bulletins I'd seen while growing up. Instead, it would be gritty, patched up, untamed, and unexplainable.

That day I didn't know this man I'd met would encourage and challenge me to walk forward in my gifts before I even believed in myself. He would see sides of me I hadn't yet recognized. His transformative story of grace would inspire me to finally tear through my Christian-good-girl facade, understand grace for the first time, and realize that my worth was in no way connected to good behavior, as I'd previously thought. I would give up some freedoms and gain new, better ones. Through his generous love, I would emerge a stronger woman, more deeply rooted in my God-given self and ready to boldly share my gifts with the world.

I didn't know the guy at the table next to me would become my best friend, workout buddy, chef, fellow farmer, adventuring companion, movie-watching partner in the "big chair," masseuse, baseball catcher, heartfelt listener, challenger, holder when I hurt, keeper of my tears, lover, father of my children, person who makes me laugh uncontrollably, and the one who still, seventeen years later, gives me chills when he puts his hand on my lower back.

I didn't yet know.

I'd been in a "friendationship" (all credit to Tara-Leigh for that word) with a guy in Nashville at the time and had recently drawn the line in the sand that our weird, nebulous friendship needed to change. He was at the conference too. Even though I loved my group of friends so much, I was growing weary of the single life—all the group hangouts with guys and girls, and even one-on-one hangouts that felt like dates, that never had the potential to move beyond friendship.

I walked around the conference that weekend in a distracted haze, trying to avoid the friendationship guy and not think too much about how frustrated I felt. I'd built a wall to protect myself against vulnerability; I was just fine on my own, thank you very much. I was blind to the realization that I'd met my future husband in the most unlikely place.

Steven and I exchanged email addresses, left the conference, and returned to our own worlds; I went to Nashville, and he went to Dallas. I wasn't close to being ready to take a risk or even *see* the possibility of a more adventurous life around the bend.

Five months later, in May 2004 . . .

Dipping my pinkie toe into the world of entrepreneurship, I had created my own website to share my watercolor artwork and some of the film photography I'd taken in Italy so I could start a little greeting card business on the side. I was also about to make a huge job change from the music and film promotions industry to work as an assistant for my photographer friend Jeremy Cowart. As was the norm in the early 2000s, I sent a mass email to all my business contacts and acquaintances to give them my new website and contact info.

In a split second before I left for lunch one day at work, I suddenly remembered "that guy in Dallas" and decided to send him the email too. No personal message, just *forward*. Send.

An hour later, a novel-like reply popped into my inbox, his response after looking through all my photos and artwork on my new website. Through his words, I sensed a man of depth who shared many of my interests and passions but who was also completely different from any guy I'd imagined dating. A half Korean who spent summers with orphans and loved Italian food, was funny and joyful yet familiar with pain, and had a charming presence that made me swoon? I mean, *come on.*

That single email, full of beautiful, life-giving words, shifted something in me—the part of me that didn't believe love would ever come for me.

I knew this was different. I just knew.

I tapped on the half wall of my office to alert Suz, whose office was on the other side, that I needed to tell her something.

"Remember that guy from Dallas we met at the conference?" I said. "I think I'm gonna marry him."

That weekend, Steven and I talked on the phone for four hours every night, putting each other on hold only for bathroom breaks. Although I didn't want to face the idea of leaving Nashville—like, *ever*—I could see how this new relationship was a huge door opening.

There was a big change coming that I knew deep in my bones was right, but my being scared to take the leap would become a theme in my life. Each time, I'd learn a little more and become braver for the next time. Although I was shaky and uncertain of the risk and unknowns, I ultimately chose to take the leap.

After a few more face-to-face visits confirmed that we were completely falling for each other, on Labor Day I found myself tearfully hugging my best friends and roommate goodbye. I drove my navy-blue Volkswagen Beetle from Nashville to Dallas to start our new life together, while Steven drove a Ryder truck stuffed with all my worldly belongings.

Since then, it's been anything but safe and ordinary, and every bit a wild, crazy journey.

After living with my big brother Glen, my sister-in-law Trish, and my toddler niece, who welcomed me into their home as I transitioned, Steven and I married in July 2005, in an outdoor ceremony in our friend's suburban Dallas backyard, by a small creek. As soon as I began walking down the "aisle"—a hill covered in rose petals—huge raindrops started to sporadically drop on my dad and me. He gripped my right hand to make sure I didn't stumble in the spongy grass while wearing kitten heels. Then, right before our vows, the clouds burst into a torrential downpour. With the unforgettable intimacy of our fifty closest friends and family members huddled around us holding polka-dotted kids' umbrellas that had been gathered from the house last minute, we spoke our vows in the beating rain. As soon as we were pronounced husband and wife, the rain stopped, and on the way to the reception, a huge rainbow arched across the sky.

Shortly after settling into married life in our rented Dallas condo with the plush maroon carpet and floor-to-ceiling mirrors, I realized something: I'd married a man who already owned a KitchenAid mixer. Cobalt blue. I think it's safe to say he'd been the only guy in his fraternity at Baylor who had one. That said, his buddies eagerly ate all the delicious things he regularly whipped up for them: batches of his gran's pound cake, from-scratch Southwestern egg rolls, and his original-recipe Yummy Cookies, which use a secret ingredient you wouldn't expect. (Sorry, friends, but he wouldn't let me put it in the book.)

When I met Steven, I thought those fancy mixers were owned only by celebrity chefs on the Food Network. Practically my entire diet consisted of things I could cook on the George Foreman Grill or in the microwave.

As much as my culinary palate was about to expand, I had no idea how much more of an adventure

I was embarking on when I chose Steven. A heart for people drew us together, and now, many years later, this shared passion is even more specific. What keeps us going on the same team (even though our personalities couldn't be more different) is a heart for creating spaces where people can feel safe, inspired, and nourished on a physical and soul level. What we're growing through that common desire has taken many forms over the years, and the roots have only grown deeper.

Ours is not an idyllic, perfect marriage. Rather, it's a marriage that's been hard-won through prayer, lots of struggle, trial and error, and wise advice from those further down the path.

In our seventeen years together, we've been through "better"—the gift of two daughters, two humble homes we've loved, business successes, supportive family, a tight community of friends. And we've been through "worse"—temporarily growing apart, losing all our money, business failures, crippling anxiety, broken relationships, and lost friendships. Through it all, two practices continue to bring freedom and connection to our marriage:

We strive to be a team, and we celebrate and respect our separateness within the team.

To borrow a phrase from our beloved marriage counselor, Doc, who declared us husband and wife that day in the pouring rain: "And the two shall become one, separately."

I truly believe marriage was meant to make us one. From the beginning, Steven and I have chosen to see that oneness, that togetherness, through the lens of a team mentality. The team is only as strong as its individual members. Great teams have opposites who balance the team.

So part of what makes our marriage work is that there's space for each of us to be as God uniquely created us, and we fight for each other to be the best version of that. This makes the team stronger.

Here's a great analogy Doc taught us: a healthy marriage is like two people Hula-Hooping at the same time. Maybe you're side by side, and your hoops might even touch or overlap sometimes. But you can't take the other person's hoop or get inside their hoop; it just won't work. You have to stay in your own hoop.

The Hula-Hoops are our individual journeys. Learning to celebrate that separateness without trying to change the other person has taken time and a whole lotta hard work.

Steven will always be a maverick: a challenger, an entrepreneur at heart who's extremely driven, fast paced, optimistic, and autonomous, living life full tilt.

I'll always be a dreamer: the calmer, slower paced, more grounded force, considering the details and others' perspectives, ultimately wanting harmony in our marriage and home.

He wants progress; I want peace. He wants to put his foot on the gas; I want to put on the brakes. But because we've committed to staying together, sometimes he needs to slow down and wait for me, and sometimes I need to trust him, jump in the car, and hold on for dear life.

Now we host outdoor farm dinners under the stars every year on our land, I'm an author (!) and farmer and homeschool teacher for our two girls, and all that time spent perfecting recipes with the cobalt-blue KitchenAid back in college paid off because Steven is a private chef for clients all over the Nashville area and is developing our own brand of artisan goods from the food we grow.

People often ask how we've been able to handle working together in addition to the challenges marriage brings. The two practices that help us work together successfully are the same ones that bring freedom to our marriage: we strive to be a team, and we celebrate and respect our separateness within the team.

Owning a farm has taken the need for a team mentality to the next level because we couldn't survive without it. I've had to buck up and do things I don't love—(wo)manhandle squawking chickens, shovel gravel, or herd runaway pigs—for the sake of the overall vision of what we're building here. Oh, and I've had to get my butt out of bed way too many early mornings to count. He enthusiastically makes sacrifices so I can still have creative outlets, like my writing and adding touches of beauty to our home and farm.

We've definitely lost it at times, and we've suffered for it. In the fledgling days of launching our businesses, I had to pull extra weight at home with small children while Steven worked insanely long hours. With all the stresses and little time to just be together, some cracks began to show in the foundation of our marriage. Communication broke down. There were misunderstandings, and there was tension. I lost my sense of self for a while, and we had to do repair work to recover so our marriage would not just survive but be an abundant one.

A few years ago, Steven and I got to have our first overnight trip together since having kids eight years before. We drove thirty minutes away from our house and then down the long, winding road to a cabin some friends graciously let us borrow for the night.

We brought our own groceries with us—our favorite Bonterra Cabernet Sauvignon and all the makings of the perfect charcuterie and cheese board with triple-cream brie, salty, crispy crackers, and Sicilian olives. The next morning, we drank creamy hot coffee in contented silence and walked through the forest, searching for wild mushrooms. Having so many hours together, undistracted, seemed luxurious.

While we were leaving for a walk before we headed back home to our girls and farm life, I took a photo of him that symbolizes our marriage so well: him standing strong, a little way ahead of me on the road, waiting patiently, not dragging me on. Meanwhile, I keep walking more slowly down the road, needing a bit of quiet encouragement to get there and knowing he'll be there to take my hand once I do.

Since that January day in Missouri, when we were brought together in the most orchestrated of ways, I've gone through probably five more Mac computers, finally embraced my curly hair, and discovered more of the separateness in my own Hula-Hoop.

I've learned that "kindred"—freedom in relationship, true connection, and a feeling of being known—can enter your life in all sorts of ways. Sometimes it's through blood. Sometimes it's through the camaraderie of a true friend. And sometimes it's through the door of a drab, gray conference hall in Branson, when a spark catches and lights up the entire room, making the first twenty-five years of your life look dim in comparison.

But there's always going to be some risk, some jumping off the edge and letting your wings catch you so you can fly.

THIS CHAPTER IS ABOUT

risk

"Kindred" can enter your life in all sorts of ways, but sometimes it will take risk, vulnerability, and a leap of faith.

- Who has lit a spark in you, lighting up the world for you in a way that feels true, in a way that you've never seen before? Who has helped you see the truest parts of your personality and celebrated your uniqueness?

- Whom will you light a spark for?

- What are some risks you've taken that were absolutely worth it?

- In what relationships do you feel most fully yourself? What is it about those relationships that makes you feel that way?

- Which people in your life feel "kindred" to you? Why?

Curry Chicken Salad

When I first met Steven, I basically lived on grilled chicken, apples, peanut butter, broccoli, and frozen chicken tenders. Thank God he swept in and showed me the whole big, beautiful world of food that was out there and helped me venture beyond bland snack food. A basic yet perfectly balanced chicken salad is one of the first recipes I learned from him, and whenever I think about it, it reminds me of our early married days, when we made this often as an easy lunch or to take on a picnic.

This recipe has both Asian and Southern flair, just like my Korean-Southern-chef husband. Duke's mayonnaise, a North Carolina staple, is a shout-out to his Southern side of the family who lives in the Raleigh area.

Makes 6 to 8 servings

1 1/2 pounds boneless, skinless chicken breast

2 cups Duke's mayonnaise or your preferred brand

1/2 cup mango chutney or peach jam

3 tablespoons curry powder

2 large celery stalks, diced small

1 1/2 cups roasted cashew halves

1/4 cup golden raisins or regular raisins

2 green onions, chopped (both the white and green parts)

2 teaspoons sea salt

1 teaspoon freshly ground black pepper

Fill a large pot with water. Put the chicken in the pot, and bring the water to a boil. Once bubbles form, reduce to a simmer, put a lid on the pot, and leave the chicken alone for 1 hour while it poaches.

While the chicken poaches, use a medium-size bowl to combine the mayonnaise, mango chutney, curry powder, celery, cashews, raisins, green onions, salt, and pepper. Stir until well combined.

Take the chicken out of the pot, and it will be fall-apart tender. Dice it into cubes, and add it to the mixture in the bowl.

SERVING SUGGESTIONS

- Garnish the chicken salad with fresh cilantro and serve it on a bed of butter lettuce or spinach.
- Stuff the chicken salad inside lettuce wraps.
- Serve the chicken salad in a bowl and use crackers or dried roasted seaweed to scoop it up.
- Spread the chicken salad on bread as an open-face sandwich.

"

There is ecstasy in paying attention. . . .

Anyone who wants to can be surprised by

the beauty or pain

of the natural world,

of the human mind and heart, and can

try to capture just that—the details, the

nuance, what is. If you start to look around,

you will start to see.

—ANNE LAMOTT,
BIRD BY BIRD

CHAPTER 3

Concrete Churches and Stunning Slums

When I think about my trip to India, I still can't believe I did it.

It was January 1, 2005. The conversations with Steven the year before at the conference about my dream to visit India one day had turned into an actual planned ten-day trip to southeast India with Peace Gospel International. I was all set to stay with my friends from Houston who had been serving there, but they'd unexpectedly returned to the States indefinitely after I'd raised funds and booked my trip. So I was going to travel all the way across the world to stay with Pastor Samuel; his wife, Pria; and their two young sons. By myself.

Steven (who was now my fiancé) had left that morning for a vacation to Kauai with his parents and sister, and I went to his condo to pack up Christmas decorations.

This trip was no longer a hypothetical—it was coming up in a week, and I was on edge. I truly wanted to be brave, to serve and finally meet the people I'd heard about from my friends who had worked with the organization, but my fear was vying for center stage. This trip to a developing nation without even a single friend by my side was guaranteed to be completely different from my previous trips to Europe and the UK as a tourist. It was so far outside my comfort zone of urban Dallas, and as much as I wanted to be adventurous, I was scared of the unknowns. Why on earth had I signed up for this? And why was I going alone?

My mom's voice kept me company on my flip phone as I carted each carefully taped box down the steep, worn carpeted stairs into the garage below Steven's condo.

Near the bottom of the stairwell, the stairs twisted to the right, and one stair was just a triangular sliver. While I was in mid-conversation, carrying the last huge carton full of fake pine-needle garland, my sock slipped on the edge of one of these twisty stairs. My feet flew out from under me, and I fell on my back—*hard*. What came out next was a jumble of cuss words that probably made my mother, who was born and bred in Jersey City, gasp. My phone went flying into oblivion, and the box with the fake garland soared through the air to land on its side at the bottom of the stairs, perfectly intact.

Groping for my phone, I called my mom back, but all I could say was, "Mommmmyyy," in a hushed, slightly panicked voice. As an inner-city pediatric nurse in New Jersey, my mom has dealt with much, much worse, so she talked me through the situation calmly and coached me how to slowly make my way back upstairs to the warmth of the apartment (as warm as any apartment can be when it's officially been stripped of Christmas cheer).

Looking back, I think she was secretly excited about the possibility that maybe now her baby girl wouldn't be getting on that plane. Although she and my dad have *always* supported me, they were less than thrilled that I was going on this solo voyage to India. I might as well have been going to live in the Amazon.

I didn't know what I'd done to my lower back, but it felt like knives were shooting through it, and part of it was numb. I could barely walk and had no earthly idea how I was going to get on a plane to India in a week.

I eventually hung up the phone, made an ice pack that could freeze a mammoth, and iced my lower back while watching episodes of *Lost* on DVD. I still remember the eerie glow of the apartment as it lit up with scenes of the stranded Losties sifting through plane crash wreckage. *Great, just what I need to watch right now.*

A few days later, there was a new development: mysterious red, itchy boils popped up in a cluster on my right palm, and I developed a swollen lymph gland in my armpit that was so sore I could barely put my arm all the way down.

While it was probably a reaction from the myriad vaccines I'd had to get for the trip, I began to wonder if I was under some sort of attack. *Okay, maybe I really shouldn't go.*

The night before I left, Steven called from Kauai to say goodbye. He had just gotten back to his hotel after hiking the Napali Coast with his sister. While he described the breathtaking scenery to me in great detail, what I really wanted to blurt out was, "Oh, *that's* nice. But I'm still getting on a plane to Asia tomorrow, my back might be broken, and I have boils."

Instead, I went for vulnerability, genuinely trying to hold back tears throughout most of the conversation. Finally, I declared what had been welling up inside for days: "I'm too scared! I can't do this. I'm not doing this."

He empathized. He encouraged. And then he showed me some tough love and said,

"Because I love you, I'm going to tell you this: the ticket is bought, and you're going. It's going to be okay."

Boarding that plane alone still goes down as one of the scariest things I've done in my life. Several hours into the twenty-one-hour plane ride, there I was, sitting in a cramped economy seat next to a male stranger and popping ibuprofen for my back pain. I was holding my backpack in a death grip because it held two very important categories of items: my protein bars and my Icy Hot patches.

I was also clutching a wooden journal that was stuffed with notes and written prayers from family and friends to give me encouragement on my solo journey. All I could do was pray. *God, I'm scared. Please be with me. And please, please, let my luggage arrive on the other side.*

At two o'clock in the morning, I made it to Chennai. While I waited at baggage claim, I anxiously scanned the crowd for Pastor Samuel and a sign with my name on it. My bag was there. *Hallelujah.*

In the customs line, I was sandwiched between Germans who had flown with me from Frankfurt and Indian mothers dressed vibrantly in saris holding children whose saucerlike brown eyes dripped with curiosity. I waited to be retrieved by Samuel and Pria, both of whom I had only seen in photos. I had no cell phone or way to reach them, just desperate prayers whispered under my breath.

Relieved, I finally found Samuel and then proceeded to violate every cultural rule in the book by flinging myself at him for a hug. I cringe even now thinking about it. The gracious man forgave me quickly, and he and Pria led me to the taxi.

My eyes were wide as I took in the first sights: people huddling under shacks on the side of the road, cows crossing the street with the cars and people steering around them like it was the most ordinary thing in the world, wild boars feeding on trash. And the colors—glorious, vibrant colors on clothes and buildings and in Hindu chalk drawings (kolams) on dirt roads in front of homes. There were splashes of beauty everywhere.

We then traveled another five hours by train to the town of Ongole, where we embraced the culture, visited children in an orphanage, brought supplies to tsunami victims, and basically were stretched in ways I never knew possible.

During the course of the trip, I went to the farthest corners of the earth, was in the most physical discomfort, saw more beautiful people, and felt more pain mingled with happiness than I ever could have anticipated. I saw the hope and joy firsthand that come from walking closely with God—the God in whom I said I believed but hadn't ever experienced like this.

"This is my work, my mission."

The words flowed from her mouth boldly yet humbly. It was late morning a few days into my trip. Every day so far, I had watched Pria clean her home, cook from scratch for multiple people, mother two young boys, take care of her jobs at their village church, and host me—a guest from America who spoke a foreign language—all with joy and a peaceful smile.

This woman was as strong as nails and also full of a spirit of tenderness that could soften every muscle in my body with the brush of her hand on my back. (You'll see.)

Here's how our daily routine went: every morning, someone in Samuel's family or ministry team delivered me a bowl of fresh boiled eggs for breakfast, and we didn't really eat anything else until the evening when we had a communal dinner together.

Daily life in India was vastly different from the way I lived in America. The first big difference was that I did not see one other white person the entire trip. I was completely and utterly the minority.

Also? Time moved so slowly. For the first few days, I felt really antsy—I was used to working out at the gym, cooking breakfast, having multiple conference calls, and answering a slew of emails all before noon.

But there, we would only do one major thing a day, like visit one of the local projects, speak at a worship service, or stuff care packages. When we did go out, every ounce of love, care, and nurture was put into those visits. Rather than constantly working from an empty or half-full vessel, the slower, simpler pace of life enabled us to pour all we had into

the many men, women, and children who would swarm us for affection, attention, and prayer.

Every evening, I sat on the floor of Samuel's home with a circle of people that included not just his wife and sons but other friends who worked in their ministry—a true picture of family. One pot of rice and a plate of naan bread were the only main meal that day for ten people. Gathering and sharing meals in this way was as much a rhythm for them as breathing.

Before we touched the meal, Samuel said prayers that left me speechless. I confess, I cracked my eyes open and peeked at his face a few times because I had never heard such sincerity. I thought that maybe if I saw his face, I would believe his words too. There was a deep reverence, a profound thanks for provision even though food wasn't always readily available and we didn't have every choice under the sun.

I had grown up learning to walk out my faith in practical ways, like feeding the homeless regularly in New York City and volunteering for local organizations with my church community. But let's be honest: my experience with Christianity was still very privileged and safe. Samuel's faith was a lifeline, clinging to hope that surpassed hunger, poverty, and unimaginable loss.

It was beyond sobering to be in southeast India near the coast a few weeks after the infamous tsunami in December 2004 that killed nearly 230,000 people. One day, we traveled for seven hours on bumpy, rugged roads in an SUV packed so full that people were riding in the trunk. I sat by the window next to Pria while she rubbed my hand for much of the trip, perhaps sensing that I was uncomfortable. Sitting that long in a truck on those treacherous roads kept sending spasms through my injured back, which was plastered to the sweaty seat. The frequent stops at rural toll booths—literally men collecting money at fold-up tables in the middle of the road—didn't help the pain.

This rugged day trip took us to a tiny, remote village near the coast, where, upon arrival, I felt like I had truly reached the ends of the earth.

The car was immediately swarmed by villagers who seemed like they'd never seen a white person before—and many of them probably hadn't. We had to drive in at a snail's pace while they traveled along with us on foot as if glued to the vehicle.

Mothers holding babies surrounded me. I used the only universal language I knew—smiles and touch. We communicated as women can across all barriers, and I stood wide-eyed, not being able to soak in their striking and weathered beauty quickly enough. They saw my digital camera and asked me to take their photos so they could see their own images.

In this village, the tsunami had just taken the lives of many of the men who were out fishing the day it hit. We delivered food, Bibles, and clothes to the widows who had just lost their husbands. One mother took the bag of rice we gave her and immediately ran to her hut to cook it for her toddler boy. He ate it while sitting on the dirt and gazing up at me.

I wanted to shut my eyes to everyone around me, and simultaneously, the thought of never seeing them again was unbearable.

In the midst of their trauma, how did these women still have vibrant smiles? Wear colorful garments? Cling to their babies with such tenderness?

The whole day was filled with so many emotions and was so far outside my comfort zone that I felt like I was watching myself from above, interacting with these unfathomably brave ones. I couldn't have felt farther away from home and my people and daily life. I pictured myself as the smallest speck in the grand, beautiful scheme of humanity.

The villagers were eager to show us around and tell us all about their lives as Pastor Samuel translated for me. While standing in a grass hut with people who'd lost husbands and fathers to the tsunami, I heard these new barefoot friends of mine talk excitedly about one thing: how proud they were to show me the new church they'd built for their village. But I didn't see a church anywhere around us.

Then I realized it was right in front of us—the church was a concrete room the size of a closet, the ceiling strewn with paper flags in shades of bright pink, purple, green, and blue. No pews, no altars, no organs, no baptismals or decorations or fancy communion wafers attached to tiny plastic wine cups. And they couldn't have been prouder. On that hard concrete floor, we sat together and sang hymns to a God who was just as much with us in the smallest village of India as in my apartment in Dallas.

I left that village forever changed. Both filled and drained and unable to ever forget their faces.

Back near Ongole, while visiting the church at Peace City, I met a widowed father of three small children. He had one leg and walked miles to church on crutches, yet he smiled freely. *Why?* I played with children at the orphanage who, through tight-eyed, earnest prayers, asked God to bless *me*. I held their hands and saw their emaciated legs carry them all around the dusty lawn where I played volleyball with them while wearing a sari. Together, we laughed and laughed.

As the days passed on, I started to notice something: rather than going to serve and help them, I was being changed. Rather than feeling disconnected from home, I felt a connection I couldn't explain as I sat on the floor with the Indian women, soaking up their essence and hearing their stories. I'd heard that joy could be present in the midst of suffering, but there, I witnessed both. I didn't understand this paradox, but I believed it for the first time in my bones.

God, what would I have missed out on if I hadn't gotten on that plane?

During my last few hours in India, Pria, Pastor Samuel, and I spent several late-night hours in a hotel room watching Bollywood shows on TV and resting before it was time for them to take me to the airport. I was wearing my sari for the last time, lying facedown on the hotel bed with my head drowsily resting sideways on my elbows.

Without a word, Pria reached out and touched my dirty, frizzy hair and ran it through her fingers. She placed her hand on my back and ran it up and down gently, over and over, sending shivers throughout my body. She must have done this for a solid hour.

I couldn't believe she was doing this. It felt shocking, even. Hadn't I come all the way here to help and serve them? Hadn't she worked hard enough already on her mission? But my injured back began to feel like it was healing, and tension from this scary, wonderful trip began to leave my body. Her touch was absolutely the hand of God to me in that moment, and I didn't want to leave her. At the same time, I was so tired and desperate for home.

This is the humbling moment I realized that this trip to India was more about what I could learn from the people I met there than what I could give them. Yes, there is an endless need for our funding and our support; I'll continue my whole life to use my voice and raise and give money to help rehabilitate women, fight human trafficking, and improve orphan and widow care. But to be face-to-face with these beautiful people, the indigenous leaders of these Peace Gospel projects, was a privilege, and they taught me more than I could ever have imagined. They are far more than capable of all the love, care, tenderness, fortitude, and faith it takes to rescue children and adults from modern-day slavery, provide for one another through poverty, and share the truest hope that shines in the midst of the deepest struggles.

I had seen a different version of the world. After the India trip, I could never unknow the things I now knew.

About six months later, I heard from my close Nashville friend Barrett Ward, who worked for an organization called African Leadership. He wanted to fly to Dallas to meet with me and tell me an idea he had—a big, urgent dream.

Over brunch at Café Brazil, Steven and I listened intently as Barrett shared his idea to build an online community for college students and young adults that would make it more doable for them to support relief projects in Africa. He wanted to call it "Mocha Club" because for just seven dollars a month, or the cost of two mochas, donors could support a relief project in Africa. This was an ask even most college students could afford, and it would make a real difference in the lives of Africans in project areas such as improving education, building schools, expanding orphan care, creating clean water wells, and providing rescue and support for women at risk and people with HIV/AIDS.

I looked down at my swirling mug of pecan-flavored gourmet coffee with half-and-half and swallowed hard.

Barrett explained that all the projects were led by indigenous Africans who were professionally trained and equipped with ongoing education and support by African Leadership. Knowing my background in grassroots marketing and street teams and my desire to be involved with people across the globe, Barrett wanted me to help him start this arm of the organization and run it alongside him, to help recruit monthly donors and equip music artists to share about the projects from the stage at their concerts.

I had left my career of seven years in the music industry and was working from home in Dallas, running a division of a faith-based marketing company that I had become acquainted with while working on *The Passion of the Christ* film the year before. We were now managing the faith-based street team for the big screen remake of *The Chronicles of Narnia: The Lion, the Witch and the Wardrobe*. While this may sound glamorous, the pressure of the film industry was getting to me; I had sat at my desk and bawled after a few of those conference calls, feeling like my skin wasn't tough enough for such a cutthroat industry. I knew it was the wrong career path for me.

So, in between bites of migas, I soaked up Barrett's every word, imagining what it would be like for my days to be spent doing work I enjoyed—with college students and musicians—while also helping make a tangible difference in meeting the needs of our global friends and helping them continue to be self-sustaining.

The decision was a no-brainer. I left the music and movie promotions industry, got married to Steven in a dreamy backyard ceremony in the pouring rain, and a week later, launched Mocha Club with our first fifty or so donor sign-ups at a Matt Wertz concert in Nashville.

The next year in October 2006, with a year of marriage and a year of helping establish Mocha Club under my belt, I was actually in Africa. I was walking down the main dirt road in Kibera, the biggest slum of East Africa in Nairobi, Kenya, with the people I'd previously seen only in photos.

I couldn't get past the burning smell at first. Whatever they're burning there in the slums—trash, wood, food—creates an aroma you don't soon forget. As I strolled down

Kibera Road with Moses and Peter, two orphaned teenage boys who lived at a youth hostel there, we passed open-air booths selling meats and vegetables.

"We heard that everyone goes to college in America. Is that true?" asked one of the boys.

I wasn't sure how to answer—it wasn't everyone, but it was definitely a vast percentage more than the children growing up on these streets. I thought about how I took many of my college studies for granted, while they were desperate for a chance to get any kind of higher schooling.

On our way to the elementary schools we were visiting, we meandered past little rivers of trash and human waste flowing quietly along the red-caked dirt road, passing half-clothed children who smiled and waved enthusiastically. There was no plumbing in Kibera, causing a stench worse than you can imagine, mixed with the smell of burning wood. The shanty shacks seemed barely big enough for two people to live in, much less families of eight or more.

The Kibera slum was hands down the most shocking place I'd ever been, and at the end of each day when we got back into the group van, all I wanted to do was stay.

What was it about that place that kept drawing me back? The activity there swirled around me, paralyzing me, stunning me. In the middle of the mess and the poverty, there was life, so much beautiful life: Doorless homes with colorful fabric hanging from the doorways. Children laughing, playing soccer at the base of a trash heap. Mamas holding naked babies protectively, with that look of fierce love in their eyes. Somehow, such contrasts existed simultaneously. I was beginning to see that Africa wasn't *only* the picture of poverty and hopelessness that's often communicated to us in the States. There was so much more there. I was captivated.

Our small team from Mocha Club visited projects in Kenya and Uganda. Children showed us their school rooms, and we played with them and fed them lunch. We held babies all day at an orphanage in Nairobi with "baby drop-off hours" posted on the front gate as if it were the most common thing in the world. We learned from workers at medical clinics and spent time with people with HIV/AIDS who made earrings and other crafts to raise money for their treatments. We even stayed at an orphanage in rural Uganda, sleeping under mosquito netting in rustic bunks and using a toilet that didn't flush.

For several weeks after I returned to Dallas, it felt like I had misplaced something. I found myself wandering around our condo aimlessly, searching for something I couldn't seem to find. Something was missing, and I was pretty sure I knew where I'd left it.

It's common to hear someone who's been to Africa say, "I left part of my heart there," with a distant look of longing in their eyes. And I never understood it, really. Sure, I left part of my heart in the magical piazzas of Venice and on the shores of the Mediterranean Sea, but in one of the world's biggest slums? At an orphanage where I wore the same clothes for three days and washed my hair in a well while a child pumped the water for me?

Yet it's true.

Today, as a mother, wife, farmer, and entrepreneur, I think of the people from halfway across the world that I carry with me.

Every fall, as I carefully build the first campfire of the season on the farm, I'm transported, and I smell Kibera in the air. On days when I've sweated through my clothes again by 10:30 a.m. or my hands are rough and bleeding from planting or my leg muscles are trembling from dragging one-hundred-foot silage tarps or I'm anxious about everything on my plate with events and responsibilities, I hear Pria's voice saying, "This is my work, my mission," and I stop in my tracks.

We think our lives are so hard and that joy is difficult to come by. But have you held hands with a woman suffering from AIDS while dancing to the beat of an African drum? I did, and I couldn't make sense of her joy until I realized that joy really does transcend. It's not *because of*; it's *regardless of.*

My life is not even close to as hard as the lives of the people I encountered in India and Uganda and Kenya. But this life is the one I have. And by declaring, "This is my work, my mission," I'm learning to own my struggles. *I can do this hard thing.* Because whatever God calls me to do, I will be equipped to do. I remember all the brave women I met. I feel Pria's love and encouragement radiating across the oceans, and I know that I'm capable of more than I think I am.

The things that connect us in our shared humanity also bring an element of difficulty, of struggle. There is no easy way to become stronger. There just isn't. If we want to become stronger and more resilient, if we want to grow, we *must* push through the hard.

But what if we say no? What if we don't get on the plane?

My trips to slums in Africa and remote villages in India changed me in ways I'm still discovering today. I constantly think of the invaluable lessons I learned there as I do my work, my mission, on the farm with my family.

Being a farmer is a commitment to build where you are, rather than wandering the earth. It's almost easier to fight against injustice and use my voice for people I don't know. But the place where I can *really* dig in? It's in the daily of my own life here.

When you decide to buy a farm, you're literally putting down roots. It's the long play, the marathon. Much of your work will not be seen for years as the topsoil grows healthier, the unseen organisms in the soil multiply, and the land slowly heals.

My whole life back then was about "go." Go into the world and do this big thing. Go help these people. Go, go, go. But now, it's "stay."

It's a vow to stay here and welcome people in. To create spaces for people to slow down and pay attention to the wild, beautiful life they're living. To be faithful with the land beneath my feet. To be a small part of a bigger story. That's just as valuable of a dream and calling. And for me, it's been much more impactful.

Halfway across the world, in the concrete churches and stunning slums, I found that the beauty of our humanity isn't defined by *where* we live but *how*. Despite the challenges of meeting their basic needs, the people I met still valued simple joys like play, music, creativity, and having the space to welcome someone in for a meal or a cup of chai. Even the humblest of abodes were sacred places of connection.

We all need lives of connection, interdependence with one another, and joy in simple things—the awe over a warm loaf of bread fresh out of the oven, the gift of music to dance to, colorful paper flags as little flashes of beauty hanging from the ceiling of a room, however otherwise stark or plain. Mothers still fiercely protect their babies. The need for food and sustenance creates vulnerability. The desire for connection is knitted into our beings. And beauty is a necessity.

THIS CHAPTER IS ABOUT

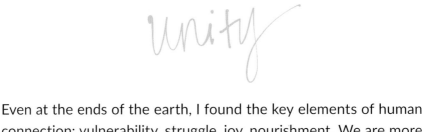

unity

Even at the ends of the earth, I found the key elements of human connection: vulnerability, struggle, joy, nourishment. We are more alike than we think we are.

- Who are some women—where you live or abroad—who have inspired you?

- How did they inspire you? How do they affect your life today?

- In your opinion, what qualities make a strong woman?

- Do you feel strong?

- I've been called to stay and sow seeds here for now. "It's a vow to stay here and welcome people in. . . . To be faithful with the land beneath my feet. . . . That's just as valuable of a dream and calling." Do you believe you can serve more effectively by being rooted to where you're called to be? How can you be faithful with the land beneath your feet today?

"

Food, a French man told

me once, is the first wealth.

Grow it right, and you

feel insanely rich,

no matter what you own.

—KRISTIN KIMBALL,
THE DIRTY LIFE

CHAPTER 4

A New Piece of Paper

Growing up in the '80s in suburban New Jersey, I watched my mom in her tube top, velour shorts, and side ponytail plant roses, lilies, black-eyed Susans, and marigolds in rubber-tire planters and window boxes. Loving the beauty and whimsy she added to our front yard and backyard but believing I had a black thumb, I only got my hands dirty when I played under my dogwood tree, Amanda, which my mom purchased and planted because I asked for a little sister. There was a spot on the lawn near Amanda where the grass was different from all the other grass—like a round, fluffy nest. My only human sibling, my brother, Glen, was nine years older, and while he took the time to play with me and watch over me when I was little, he was already a million miles away at college in West Texas. So I often found solace in nature and freedom to explore the worlds inside my imagination. When I wasn't at the pool with my parents, riding bikes with my mom, or at a friend's house around the corner, I loved playing pretend under that tree, in that little suburban yard overlooking the baseball fields. I literally hugged trees. I studied the oak leaves and evergreens, pretending I was gallivanting through an enchanted forest, lost in imaginary worlds, and always wooed by beauty.

In elementary school, which I walked to every single day with my friend Jason, I loved art class with a passion. I lived for the moments spent each week in that classroom at the end of the hall, tucked away as if it were an afterthought. The art room was like the center of everything in my world and where all my senses came alive: the scent of tempera paints dried around the rims of the plastic containers, the texture of prickly brushes crammed into a mason jar, the feel of tissue paper as thin as poppy petals. And the colors. Bright colors, lots of colors, millions of possibilities, like a handful of wildflower seeds.

But even in third grade, I wanted all of my artistic outpourings to be perfect, or at least perfect to me. I wanted them to come out exactly as I saw them in my mind. When they didn't come out that way and I needed to start fresh, I loved the freedom of asking for a new piece of paper.

That freedom is what I love about growing things; it's what I love about growing a life.

What I only mildly understood as a child in art class is now one of the most liberating recurring themes of my adult life: we are free to change and grow and say, "Nope, that doesn't work for me anymore," without apology or justification. We are free to move on. We are free to re-create a new, abundant life with the tools God has given us to tend, cultivate, invite, gather, nourish, and enjoy.

Whether it produces a few herbs in pots on an apartment balcony or an entire hundred-foot row of lettuce resembling bouquets of bright-green roses, gardening is forgiving. We start with a blank piece of paper, fill it up, try out colors, textures, variations. And then, each year after the last frost, we get a new canvas with which to begin again.

The dreaming, planning, expectation, opportunity for a fresh start—these are my favorite things about gardening, and now farming on a larger scale.

Thankfully, I now know that perfection isn't an option; it's not even possible. Living on a sustainable farm where animals, soil, pollinators, vegetables, and weather variables are all part of a brilliant ecosystem that works together so intricately, we know that one thing out of our control can affect all the others. For example, if the nectar doesn't flow as well for the bees one season, there's not enough honey for us to harvest from the hive, or if the bees get sick from chemical spray on nearby industrial farms or are attacked by moths, we don't have enough pollinators for our fruits and vegetables. One season, we'll have the most incredible cherry tomatoes we've ever grown—perfect orbs that burst open into little golden sunshines. And the next season, the tomatoes seem to be struggling and, despite our best sustainable efforts, are riddled with pests.

Oh, if only I could get back the countless hours of my life I've wasted trying to make something perfect rather than enjoying the beautifully messy process and the imperfect end result. I'd love to tell that little girl in art class to tear up more paper. To get messier. To keep her eyes on the work of her own hands rather than others' expressions of approval or disapproval. I'd love to tell her about the beauty that unfolds—courage, adventure, joy—when we rise up to challenges and say yes to lives of risk and change.

In 2006, a big change started unfolding. Steven had left his job at 963 Missions, and we'd become business partners in a holistic exercise and wellness studio in Dallas with our friends who were personal trainers. Steven handled the business and marketing side while I was still working full-time for Mocha Club. I fell in love with my yoga mat, and in the evenings after work, we met up with our friends at their gym and learned how to strengthen our bodies through primal movements with kettle bells, do walking lunges down the hallway holding giant watercooler bottles, and refuel after our workouts by gulping down cups of whey protein from grass-fed cows.

We learned from them how to live healthier lives centered around functional exercise and real, unprocessed foods, but it was a slow, gradual journey. I remember saying to them one day, "There is no way I will ever *not* put Splenda in my coffee." I didn't realize then there was another healthier, more holistic way and that I could treat my body better by eating foods as close as possible to their natural state, as they were created.

I still remember what it tasted like when I first bit into an organic apple. I was shocked because I suddenly realized I'd never actually *tasted* an apple before. I'd heard about things like kale and collard greens, and discovered that beets could actually be incredibly tasty and not at all like the magenta rubbery nuggets in steak house salad bars. Each little step seemed monumental at the time, like when we started taking probiotics and giving up soft drinks for kombucha.

I absorbed every word in the books *The Maker's Diet* by Jordan Rubin and *Nourishing Traditions* by Sally Fallon and put their suggestions into practice as we gradually reformed our eating habits, pickling and fermenting things in jars on the countertop and learning how to make delicious recipes with these "new" ancient foods. I looked at what I was eating and couldn't believe the progression. *I just had flax seed on berries with my breakfast, and my new favorite dessert is frozen hemp milk sandwiched between two hemp cookies. What the . . . ?*

I did have limits, though. After an unfortunate episode where a spirulina algae capsule exploded in my throat at work one day, causing my mouth to taste like a pond for the next twelve hours, it was a while before I could venture back into green superfoods. I also drew the line with a few of the *Nourishing Traditions* recipes, like "brains in wine sauce" and "sweetbreads" (which I had only heard of because of a question in the game Cranium).

But overall, I had exponentially more energy, started sleeping like a rock, and couldn't wait to dive further into this newfound world of real, nourishing food. *Small* changes in our lifestyle were beginning to have such a *huge* impact.

I couldn't help but wonder—could we actually grow real food ourselves in the middle of the city?

In spring 2006, while we were still living in our urban condo under a city overpass, we borrowed a friend's backyard where he generously allowed us to dig up a patch of soil and plant some vegetables.

Bless our hearts, we were so desperate to grow something—*anything*—that we drove across Dallas a few times a week just to visit and water our fragile seedlings. I'm almost positive we had no idea what we were doing then, and no matter what happens now, it has to be better than harvesting *one single cucumber*, which is all we got in the summer of 2006.

Yes, friends, a single cucumber. I have the photo to prove it.

It's so easy to throw in the towel, to just be defeated—at least for my personality that prefers peace over conflict and the status quo over the unknown. But a seemingly small decision at the end of that season was pivotal. We would start again with a new piece of paper.

In the fall of 2006, we purchased our first home—a 1920s mint-green just-restored Craftsman-style bungalow in an artsy urban Dallas neighborhood called Oak Cliff. There was an industrial warehouse across the street, a Mexican bakery on one corner, and a liquor store on the other. A true haven for us from the moment we moved in, that home was the precious place where, for nine years, we grew our marriage, food, flowers, babies, and friendships.

As soon as we were handed the keys on a sunny October morning, I, ever the dreamer and idealist, was absolutely giddy. I couldn't wait to paint every single wall a different color, get a dog, make a Pinterest-inspired guest room headboard out of plywood and fancy fabric, and set up a fair-trade coffee and tea bar in the kitchen for our morning lattes.

And oh, the backyard. Although we lived the city life, worked full-time, and didn't have tons of space, I couldn't help but wonder what possibilities would grow there.

I stood on the back steps overlooking our positively blank piece of Texas soil (all ours!): a perfect grassy square bordered by a brand-new wooden privacy fence.

On one side of us were neighbors who had questionable meetings at the curb through the cracks in their slightly rolled-down driver's side windows and a backyard filled with massive piles of trash and dogs on chains. The neighbor on the other side was a friendly Spanish-speaking artist and sculptor who, at the time, held a Guinness World Record for creating the largest bowl of guacamole. No kidding.

Sandwiched between the two of them, we went to work transforming our little piece of urban green space.

I knew one thing: I wanted flowers. Lots of 'em.

That fall, a fire pit and some tiki torches were the best we could do.

The next spring, in 2007, we started with a tiny postage stamp–size square-foot garden, and all we grew that season were some marigolds and a few sad-looking tomatoes. But we grew *something*.

Then, on Christmas Day 2007, taking advantage of the mildness of Texas winter, we *really* went after it. I had just turned thirty and made a list of "37 Things I Want to Do By the Time I Turn 37" (yup, so random). On the list was "Grow a flower garden in my own backyard." Because landscape edging isn't cheap, you know, we started digging up the old, decrepit brick patio to form flower beds.

I wrestled weeds so fierce they bit back, cutting my arms, and others so stubbornly rooted that I was knocked to the ground, left with only a few shredded leaves in my fist. And oh, the "treasures" we unearthed—decades of debris: old pieces of shag carpet, bent spoons, plastic action figures, and even a cat skull.

We built makeshift wildflower beds with the bricks all along the fence and sowed seeds that I (crossing my fingers) hoped would grow into something beautiful. The packet said the seeds would take seven days to sprout. Every morning, I expectantly crept into the yard, first waiting for the slightest sprout of green, then examining new shoots to see whether they were flower sprouts or weeds, and finally seeing what I thought were *actual real flowers* that had popped up overnight. It was the simplest of joys and something I looked forward to every day.

The only problem? I had no idea what weeds looked like. And guess what, my friends? That wildflower bed was about 99 percent weeds.

Turns out, planting wildflowers in the shade isn't ever going to work. And soil that's never grown anything but grass needs to be amended with compost and fertilizer first so it's full of the nutrients that help plants and flowers grow.

I kind of want to hug my naively proud thirty-year-old self who just wanted to grow something beautiful in her backyard and admire tiny poppies unfurling their pointed heads every morning while she stood admiring them in her red gardening Crocs.

I'm so glad I didn't know everything then, because a deep hopefulness kept me going. And we must have hope if we're going to try.

Actually, I believe that choosing to *grow something*—a garden, a family, a career, a life—is one of the most hopeful stances we can have.

It takes vulnerability to take a step when *only that step* on the path is lit and the rest of the path ahead appears dark. Even though we don't know what's coming or where it'll lead, choosing to grow means we move forward a little bit and see what unfurls. I don't know about you, but I'd rather be the person who took that first step than the one sitting on the sidelines, hopeless and dreamless, wondering what could have unfolded.

So what about that first attempt at growing wildflowers? I enjoyed the few that were able to push through (and took a bazillion photos of them for my blog), but eventually the garden was overtaken by weeds.

The next gardening season, armed with newfound knowledge, we tried again to grow more flowers and food, adding several raised beds surrounded by cedar mulch walking paths. Little by little, our imperfect "backyard homestead," as we began to call it, took shape. Building and growing something from scratch taught me so much about hope.

I was hopeful that the time Steven and I spent building this beautiful thing together would be an investment into our marriage and into the people we loved, who would finally get to exhale and relax in the red hammock next to the lilies after a tough day.

I was hopeful that we'd be able to create a comforting meal for someone with the tomatoes and basil and peppers we grew from a seed starter in the dead of winter.

I was hopeful that our labor would turn into something useful—and beautiful.

In the garden, there was something for both of us. I spent quiet hours with my own thoughts, much like those moments in art class when the entire classroom was hushed and hovered over their pieces of paper. I saw another facet of Steven's usually boisterous personality as he diligently and meticulously planted vegetable seeds.

Although on really tiring days I wished our garden pruned and weeded itself, the satisfaction that came from harvesting enough vegetables to make an entire crunchy, colorful salad from our very own backyard was worth every bit of effort. I spent every day doing some life-giving work in the garden. The time and care we put into it only made the arugula taste spicier, the tiny pole beans sweeter.

Our kitchen counters began to be piled with the bounty, and every day there was a new harvest: Loads of herbs such as mint, green and purple basil, oregano, sage. Fistfuls of red onions. Red cherry tomatoes and tiny golden heirloom pear tomatoes. Adorable pea pods. Fuzzy okra, shiny green bell peppers, and spiny canning cucumbers that were crunchier than any I'd tasted before. Handfuls of luscious, tart blackberries. Swiss chard, arugula, collard greens. Sweet potato vine that we sprouted by sticking a sweet potato in the ground and watering it. Fancy-sounding lettuces like "craquerelle du midi" and "cook's mesclun mix." Squash as big as baseball bats, which we learned to slice thinly with a mandolin and eat raw in a salad. And more flowers—cosmos, poppies, sweet alyssum, coneflowers, and sunflowers.

A whole lot more than a single cucumber.

Soon, there were so many tomatoes that they took over the entire back quarter of our yard, and we figured we could probably feed the entire street if we wanted to. We joked that maybe we should start our own produce co-op.

We celebrated all the food produced by the work of our hands and the blessings of earth, wind, and rain. The whole place hummed with color and life. Our garden was a home for birds, a haven of rest, the backdrop for laughter around a campfire, a place where hymns were sung and guitars strummed, and even the site of a first kiss and marriage proposal in the red hammock, which thereafter became known as the Red Hammock of Love.

There were plenty of blunders and plenty of struggles, but we kept going. We composted, dug, planted, weeded, pruned, prayed for rain, and had a moment of silence for our beloved pole beans that shriveled up and died a few weeks after the first harvest.

We learned what worked and what didn't. Each season, we took out our new piece of paper and tried again.

By cultivating our own little patch of beauty nestled between our home and three sides of a fence, we were doing our part to redeem and reclaim the earth, little by little.

Then, something else was birthed. We had a little girl, Luci. The joy of having a backyard full of growing things was exponentially better with little hands to dig in the soil.

But not at first.

When we first became parents in the summer of 2010, our garden stood neglected in the relentless Texas heat. It was all we could do to survive life with a newborn in the 107-degree Dallas summer. Scorched grass and weeds took over the area where we'd put in so many years of hard work.

This was it—the pivotal moment we all face where we have to choose: Will we muster every bit of courage and keep going? Or will we listen to the voices of doubt and fear that tell us it's all too hard, that it's not worth the effort?

Again, a new piece of paper. We dug in, this time refreshing the whole landscape of the yard and adding a fluffy grass lawn in the middle, surrounded by perennial flower beds and good-quality, long-lasting cedar raised beds for veggies in the back. As a toddler, our oldest daughter loved sitting on the dirt inside the raised beds of tomatoes, giggling deviously as she plucked off the green ones.

We added a few chickens—Butter, Licorice, and Tulip. And then a few years later, our second daughter, Norah, joined our family. We planted a fairy ring with gladiolus bulbs where she loved to sit and play. As Luci grew, she loved checking on the blackberry bushes each morning and making bouquets with wildflowers and surprising me with them from behind her back.

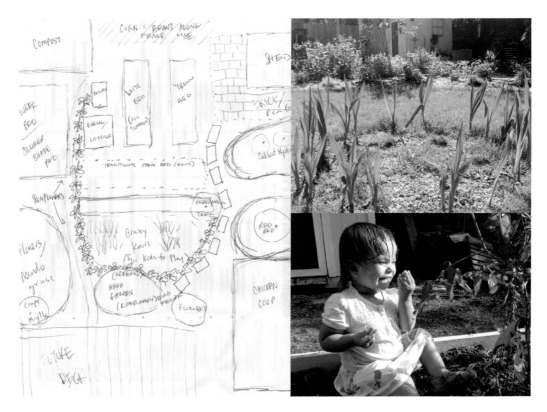

One spring, six seasons into creating our backyard homestead, I wrote this in my journal:

> What's never changed is our dream to have our own farm one day—not in the city, but just outside a small city (Nashville?)—where we grow delicious organic food and host farm dinners at a big rustic table on a patio with white twinkle lights and our children grow up frolicking freely in fields of flowers and horses and goats and chickens. It's a wonderful, worthy dream, but if we cannot grow food in our small urban backyard in Dallas, we surely won't be able to grow it on forty acres of land. Anywhere.

Today, we have seventeen acres but no horses or goats (yet), and my oldest daughter is not a fan of chickens chasing her around. But this overall vision *did* happen—all the way down to the farm dinners with white twinkle lights. Not because of some lofty pipe dream but because we risked and failed and tried again.

The Jersey girl who believed she had a black thumb as a child and watched her mom plant roses and marigolds is now an organic produce farmer growing thousands of tomatoes and heads of lettuce and flowers each season.

And it's all still unfolding. Now, so many years later, every single time a seed sprouts,

I have the same feeling of awe: it actually *worked*. Growing things helps you to never lose your sense of wonder.

It's a miracle every single time.

Last year, for the first time, we planted an entire field of perennial and annual wildflowers behind the greenhouse on top of the hill. One Saturday, when the wildflowers and zinnias were absolutely bursting with color, we decided to open up the fields for u-pick.

While we always sell jars of freshly picked flower bouquets at our farm store, there's a difference between *buying* a flower bouquet and *interacting* with the flowers. I wanted people to have a tactile experience—to have the opportunity to slow down, connect with nature, be creative, and decide what they thought was beautiful.

We weren't sure what to expect. At nine o'clock that morning, multiple cars pulled in the driveway, and the flow kept coming. All morning long, there were men, women, and children of all ages traipsing around the flowers, putting together bouquet combinations, and harvesting flowers for friends. An older couple. A mom with a newborn baby. A child who picked flowers and then gave me a donation of coins that she'd earned from her own lemonade stand. The joy was palpable.

What started as a dream in a Dallas backyard, with a whole lot of small steps forward over time, grew to an acre of organic produce bursting with abundance and wildflowers stretching to the sky, teeming with people, bees, and butterflies.

But if I hadn't tried and gone for something that was on my dream list way back then, growing this field of magic wouldn't have been as meaningful.

When I saw all those flowers sprawled out before everyone, my first thought wasn't, *Wow, look at all we've built here.*

It was the image of that first, single cucumber so many years ago and the couple who had no clue what they were doing. It was a snapshot of that hopeful girl in her tiny fledgling urban garden with all the weeds, admiring a single poppy in her gardening Crocs.

She had enough courage to try.

Is there something you've always wanted to do, but you've been afraid to go for it? Maybe it's time.

If you and I were in person right now, I'd take your hand and give it a little squeeze and remind you of this because it's something I believe with every fiber of my being:

Starting small is okay.

Starting small is good.

Start small, but just begin.

Because you're free as a bird, my friend. You're free to change and grow. You're free to let go of the things that aren't working for you anymore.

If, and *when*, you mess up, that's okay. Just clear the land, amend the soil, and start again.

And the best part?

You're a grown-up now, so you don't even have to ask for a new piece of paper. Just take it—and start painting.

THIS CHAPTER IS ABOUT

We all have to start somewhere, and we're all amateurs at the beginning. We can't let that stop us. Until we try, we never know what goodness might unfold. Start small. Just begin.

- What is something that is definitely not working for you anymore?

- What is your "new piece of paper"?

- What dream, goal, or idea do you have in mind right now?

- What's holding you back from trying for the first time or trying all over again?

Here are some steps to take:

- **Clear the land.** What in your life needs to be eliminated so you can purse this dream?

- **Amend the soil.** Add in nourishment by surrounding yourself with voices and knowledge that move you closer to your purpose.

- **Start small; just begin.** You're not building an entire farm yet, just a tiny garden. How can you take the first small step forward?

Signature Tea and Coffee Lattes

This is exactly how I've been making my tea and coffee drinks for years, and it always transports me back to my Dallas backyard garden, where I loved to drink a morning tea or coffee latte and walk around, dew collecting on my shoes, to see what had sprouted overnight.

Now I like drinking a morning latte while visiting the wildflower fields and saying good morning to my lettuce plants and cosmos reaching to the sun.

If you come to my house, you'll be offered one of these, and you'll get to choose your favorite mug too.

When I make a tea latte, I use yerba maté, which is a loose-leaf tea made with leaves grown in the South American rainforest and hand harvested. It's loaded with vitamins, minerals, antioxidants, and polyphenols. Yerba maté is brewed into a tea and savored every day in many South American countries, preferably with friends. It gives you natural energy from "mateine," which doesn't cause the same jittery effect of caffeinated coffee.

Still, I'm not completely giving up coffee! When I make a coffee latte, I make it in a French press. I like a medium or dark roast because it makes richer coffee drinks.

Makes 1 serving

1 (13.5-ounce) can coconut milk
1/4 cup filtered water
12 ounces brewed yerba maté or brewed coffee
1 packet or 8 drops natural sweetener
Sprinkle of cinnamon

In a mason jar, add the coconut milk and filtered water, then shake vigorously. (I find that undiluted coconut milk is great for cooking but too rich to drink in a latte.) You could also warm the coconut milk in a pan with 1/4 cup filtered water until it's combined. Put the thinned coconut milk in a jar and store in the fridge for later use.

Brew the tea or coffee according to your preferred method and strength.

Froth about ¹/₄ cup of the thinned coconut milk. I have an electric frother that both heats and froths the milk. If you don't have one of these, then froth it with a handheld frother.

Choose your mug, add sweetener to the bottom of the mug, and pour in the hot tea or coffee.

Layer the frothed milk on top and sprinkle with cinnamon.

NOTES

- You can substitute another nut milk, but coconut milk is my favorite. If you use a different milk, there's no need to thin it with water.
- Stevia is my preferred natural sweetener. I use either 1 packet of powdered or 8 drops of SweetLeaf Sweet Drops Vanilla Crème liquid stevia. However, if you don't like the taste of stevia, you can substitute 1 tablespoon of honey, maple syrup, or coconut palm sugar.

"

The safest dreams we experience are

dreams with no hope of coming true . . .

Concrete dreams, on the other hand, are based

on effort and a keen sense of what is possible.

Concrete dreams juxtapose the

what if with the maybe,

they expose us to hope and to

risk at the very same time.

Living with the possible takes guts.

—SETH GODIN,
WHAT TO DO WHEN IT'S YOUR TURN
(AND IT'S ALWAYS YOUR TURN)

CHAPTER 5

Texas Back Roads in a Volkswagen Rabbit

While watching the documentary *Food, Inc.* one evening in 2009 in the comfy two-seater chair in our Dallas living room, Steven and I stared at the TV screen wide-eyed. With gorgeous cinematography and golden-hour footage of cattle happily grazing in bright-green grassy meadows, the film features the story of farmer Joel Salatin and Polyface, his family's thriving, two-thousand-acre multigenerational farm in the Shenandoah Valley of Virginia. Through organic and sustainable farming practices, they've built a six-figure business and helped define the "locavore" movement, which encourages people to support as many local farms and artisans as possible with their food choices.

Food, Inc. shined a light on corporate farming in the United States and how the big machine of industrial agriculture continues to produce unhealthy food, using chemicals and practices that are harmful to people, animals, and the environment. Many organic farmers in the US are suffering and struggling on their own while trying to help people connect to the land and provide them with real, nutritious produce and meat from healthy animals.

By the time the film finished, I was shocked and outraged. Organic and sustainable farmers were using ancient practices (from way before the industrial revolution arrived) that contributed to healing the environment and people's health. Yet these farmers were seen as abnormal, weird, or on the fringes. *Why?* All the while, chemically sprayed produce required that the land be stripped of life by industrial farming practices. Animals were being severely mistreated at factory farms and feedlots, and this was all being sub-sidized by the US government while organic farmers struggled.

It was a pivotal moment that woke us both up big time. We were suddenly and shock-ingly aware of the massive problems in the food system and how we were contributing to it as consumers. We had never been so aware of how much the way we spent our dollars *mattered*.

At the time, Steven was still working with our friends who had the holistic exercise and wellness studio, I was still working for Mocha Club, and we didn't have any children yet. Just as I had experienced in my awakening during my trips across the globe, once again I found myself in a situation where I couldn't unknow the things I now knew. Would I sit on this new information, or would I change?

The desire to be a part of the change led to inspiration. I thought of the purity of the little backyard garden we were in the midst of building—the shiny basil leaves and tomatoes and peas that were safe to pluck and eat straight off the vine. I thought of how much it already meant to us and so many others. How could we move beyond our backyard to a wider activism?

We did the first thing we could think of: look up who our local farmers were. *Who grows organic produce within a fifty-mile radius of us?* We began to passionately pursue organically and sus-tainably grown food from local farmers at the grocery store and researched which farms we could visit so we could purchase directly from them.

Plus, the idea of escaping the city on the weekend sounded really appealing.

So we filled the entire hatchback of our tiny, trusty green Volkswagen Rabbit (which had recently replaced my beloved blue Beetle) with a giant cooler and hit the Texas back roads. This became our new favorite Saturday morning pastime: visiting local farms to pick up raw milk with the cream on top, fresh eggs, sourdough bread still warm out of the oven, organic berries, homemade raw cheddar cheese, and sweet potatoes with dirt still on them.

Driving away from the city and toward farmland and a simpler way of life was some-thing we began to call "That Saturday Morning Feeling."

We loved meeting these brave farmers and learning about their worlds, their passions, and what they had to offer. And all week long, we looked forward to experiencing that peace and fulfillment again.

Armed with travel mugs, we usually left the house at 7:30 a.m. to embrace the chilly morning. With the Dallas skyline in the rearview mirror and the never-ending Texas horizon sprawled in front of us, I'd exhale.

I had no idea what was coming next—I just knew I loved these weekend mini road trips, venturing out of the concrete jungle into the wide-open spaces. A momentary escape from traffic and the hustle of city life. A chance to breathe fresh air. Three-hundred-sixty-degree beauty and a slower pace.

These were exactly what my soul *craved*.

Full Quiver Farms was the first farm we ever visited together. It was a one-hour drive from Dallas, in Kemp, Texas, a tiny town with a smattering of antique shacks on the side of the road, a tanning salon, a Pennsylvania Dutch store, and some gas stations. The farm was operated by a friendly Mennonite family—a mother, Debbie; a father, Mike; and their nine children.

As soon as we pulled up the gravel drive, Debbie emerged from her farmhouse, the wooden screen door clapping behind her. She wore a long dress that grazed the ground, her hair tied back simply in a covered bun.

Always full of vibrancy as she shared about her family and the farm, Debbie told us stories about her life that spoke volumes, such as that there would be thirty-seven guests, including all the children and grandchildren, at their family's upcoming Thanksgiving feast (the same exact menu every year). She said they tried to go on a family vacation once, but they couldn't wait to get back home to the farm and simply sit together in the pasture around a warm fire.

They grew, made, or raised everything they ate or sold right there on their slice of Texas soil. The only reason they went to the grocery store was for salt, pepper, and oatmeal.

This farming family's life was built around hard work, consistency, and determination but also much joy. We soaked it up each Saturday, peppering them with questions while swooning over the pungent homemade cheeses and stuffing as much freshly baked sourdough as possible into our shopping basket. *Mmm . . . can't wait to toast that with butter and make some bruschetta with tomatoes and basil from the garden later.*

Our cooler now bursting with farm-fresh goodies in the back of our Rabbit, we left with renewed priorities and perspectives—and grumbling stomachs. We couldn't *wait* to share this with our friends. Once we got home, we'd scramble to unload the cooler, bust open the bags of warm, squishy bread, and invite some friends over for brunch.

As soon as we showed them our spoils, they wanted in on the farm's offerings. Farm-fresh eggs fried in coconut oil, the yolks bright-orange and creamy. Organic Texas cantaloupe slices with sweet juice that dripped down your hands. Savory pasture-raised sausage crack-

ling in the pan. Homemade Russian black bread slathered in grass-fed butter and drizzled with local raw honey.

Once our friends tasted that food, there was no turning back. So they started placing orders: "Hey, will you grab me a gallon of raw milk, some fresh butter, and a loaf of sour-dough while you're there?"

Soon, we were pushing the limits of what our little hatch-back could hold, with not only the trunk but also the back seat stuffed to the gills. Our trusty green Rabbit had never seen so much action as she kept zipping up and down the Texas back roads.

After we got the goods from the farms on Saturdays, we would often drop by the training studio for a kettle-bell workout. Now the clients were curious. Word quickly spread, and others wanted us to bring back farm goodies too. Before we knew it, we were distributing this nutritionally dense, beautifully raised food to friends and *their* friends.

We started to get so many orders that we decided to set up a bunch of coolers in a cen-tralized pickup location in the only place that made sense: the parking lot of the training studio, smack-dab in the middle of Dallas off North Central Expressway.

And that's essentially how our future was born in a random Dallas parking lot. Within a handful of months, "a few friends and clients" turned into seventeen families, and we had unknowingly started our very own organic food co-op.

Having a posture of curiosity, a posture of learning, is so crucial to being open and available to whatever our lives hold next. The desire to actually *learn* from these farmers and soak up their wisdom—not just pick up our food and leave—led to the next stage of our lives and a business we never could have imagined when we first started driving those Texas back roads.

Of course, we didn't know then what was coming down the pipeline—that we were building a business that would eventually have thirty-five employees and lead us to work nearly round the clock for years to spread our collective passion of local, organic, and sustainable food all throughout the Dallas–Fort Worth area.

If I had, I probably would've quit right then and there. I'm not a born entrepreneur like Steven; I've learned, slowly, how to be one. My brain doesn't naturally see numbers and profits and business growth potential. "Going big" and taking risks kinda scares me because of all the what-ifs, the details, the potential roadblocks. Thank God he was there, cheering us on and moving us forward to say the brave *yes*.

But you know what *did* light me up? Gathering people together in parking lots to distribute nourishing food from hardworking farmers and seeing how happy they were.

The excitement over what they had ordered from the farms was palpable. People conversed about food and recipes, shared stories of bodies healing and getting healthier, and were able to engage more fully in the lives they loved.

Connection and community were growing and blooming before our eyes. I never would have imagined that this would all begin from a simple Saturday morning road trip.

As our little parking lot co-op kept growing, we had to make decisions on the fly and enlist friends to help us sort the produce into shares. We also needed to source more and more produce from local farms, so we asked farmers to start growing items just for us. We didn't need just a *few* bundles of turnips or radishes or collards anymore, but *fifty* or a *hundred*.

At this point, our farm visits became much more personal as we got to really invest time with the farmers and develop a relationship with them. We learned farming methods and were able to get our hands dirty planting and harvesting too. This was integral since we were the ones who needed to be accountable to our co-op members and friends about what we were sourcing.

One overcast morning, which was incredibly welcome after a scorching Texas summer, we visited Eden Creek Farm in Blooming Grove, Texas, population 847. The gray canopy of coziness followed us our entire one-hour drive from Dallas deeper and deeper into the country. As we entered the dirt road leading to the farm, our car wound through evergreens and mesquite trees, and unsure of what would await us around the next turn, I began to feel like we were entering some sort of fairytale land. Finally, the road opened into a clearing where there stood not a wide-porched farmhouse, but a huge gray adobe home—totally unexpected.

The farming couple, the Orths, welcomed us inside and offered us steaming cups of dark-roast coffee as we sat in their living room filled with the warming scents of incense and wood burning in the stove. Then, in our Crocs, boots, and tennis shoes, we began traipsing around the farm for a tour, but not without stopping to visit their rescued pet squirrel, who enjoyed belly rubs.

As their German shepherd led us through the forest, the Orths guided us on what was safe to eat along the way. We paused to stoop down and forage tart wild plums, sweet wild persimmons, lemon mint, and edible hibiscus that tasted like fresh oranges.

And then—I'll never forget this—as we rounded a bend in the forest, suddenly four unbridled, majestic horses emerged from amid the trees as if from a scene out of *The Lord of the Rings*. As they grazed on the forest floor, we were allowed to pet them and give them snacks, and I was absolutely enamored.

Along the tour, we got to help with harvesting, and the Orths gathered a variety of items for us to take home and enjoy, including a squash that was so long it wrapped around my neck like a boa constrictor.

As we drove home, I felt a deep satisfaction—one foot there on the rural soil, captivated by the quieter, simpler way they lived, and one foot in my own urban backyard, excited to continue creating a piece of the simple life right where we were.

Something fun to do on a Saturday morning changed our lives when we decided we wanted to live more connected—to nature, to the source of our food, and to each other—while still living in a big, bustling city.

With a whole lot of grit, scrappiness, and hard work, we were able to grow from seventeen families picking up bins of produce in a parking lot to a citywide organic produce co-op that served 2,300 families all over the Dallas–Fort Worth metroplex. Eventually, it became our own organic market and café and quarter-acre urban farmstead with chickens, rabbits, aquaponics, and bees on the roof.

All because of the farmers whose hands we had shaken, whose land our feet had touched.

These are just a few of the farmers whose names are permanently seared into the soil they have tended and nurtured:

- Brenton at Johnson's Backyard Garden
- Garrett and Stacie at Gundermann Acres
- Jon and Wendy at Burgundy Pasture Beef
- Mike and Connie at Windy Meadows
- Dan at Yellow Prairie

And their names are now seared into some of my absolute best memories for the ways they impacted my life.

From Jim and Kay at Richardson Farms, we learned about animal welfare as they raised turkeys for us and let us visit them so we could be more connected to where our food came from.

Jacky and Cindy at Morrison Organic Farm worked tirelessly to grow beautiful organic produce for our co-op, and to this day I have no idea how they did it all—growing thousands of pounds of produce for us every year, just the two of them. When we drove out to their farm to visit them, they served us hot muffins one still-dark, early morning.

With Eric and Karen at Caprino Royale, we sat under shade trees after touring their goat farm, eating crackers and a trio of the creamiest chèvre, which came from the milk of their beloved goats bleating just a few feet away.

Some of the family farms we built a relationship with back then are still flourishing, and some haven't survived, as is often the reality. But in my life, they made an indelible imprint. They were just doing their jobs diligently with passion—they didn't know the time they spent with us was stoking the fire of a dream that would continue to grow for years to come.

I now know there are faces behind every single bundle of organic greens, every apple, every carrot, every tomato, and I feel so honored to have learned that profound truth firsthand from these farmers who are truly heroines and heroes.

I may not have known for sure back then that I wanted to be a farmer, but I knew the fulfillment of growing things, and I was drawn to a slower, simpler, more sustainable way of life. If I hadn't walked down the path—or driven down the road—I wouldn't have known that something unique and special was just around the bend.

Let's not wait until the time is right or the scenario is perfect or all the ducks are in a row.

Let's not sit around wondering if anything will ever come of our God-breathed dreams or, even worse, stifle and stuff them deeper and deeper down inside.

We can't afford to spend another minute making excuses about why we haven't pursued the unique gifts we have to contribute goodness to the world.

I believe in your journey and what you have to offer. I believe you can do something right now to move in the direction of change toward the passions quickening your heart and bubbling up inside you:

Grab a friend, get in the car, and start heading down the back roads.

Keep your eyes open.

Explore.

See where each road leads.

Regardless of the destination, at least you'll know you explored the possibility, and that's something you'll never, ever regret.

THIS CHAPTER IS ABOUT

exploration

When we pay attention to the passions bubbling up inside us, then explore them regardless of the destination, we can create something special and unique.

- Think about how the farmers invited us into their way of life and made time for us to learn. "They were just doing their jobs diligently with passion—they didn't know the time they spent with us was stoking the fire of a dream that would continue to grow for years to come." Has someone done that for you?

- How can you live in such a way that it might stoke the fire of another person's dreams?

- What is something you've been wanting to explore? Whom can you take with you?

- What "back roads"—places you can visit or research, or people you can talk with—would help you learn more about the dream or idea you're wanting to pursue?

Heirloom Tomato Bruschetta

I can taste them now as I type this: sweet, tangy heirloom tomatoes carried home in a little paper basket from a Texas farm trip that morning, which means those tomatoes were probably pulsing on the vine the day before. Fresh basil from our backyard garden, pungent Parmesan cheese, and the juices dripping as my teeth sink into the thick, buttery toasted bread.

Making this recipe with our own farm-grown tomatoes now is even more fulfilling. It's as simple and rustic as it gets, yet it is a stunner on a plate.

Makes 4 servings

2 large heirloom tomatoes, diced
2 teaspoons sea salt
4 tablespoons extra virgin olive oil, divided
4 large, thick slices sourdough bread
1 large garlic clove, minced
1 cup grated Parmesan cheese, divided, plus more for garnish
1 tablespoon red wine vinegar
6 large basil leaves, cut into thin ribbons, plus more for garnish

Place a colander over a large bowl. Put the diced tomatoes in the colander and sprinkle with the sea salt. Mix and let the tomatoes sit in the colander for 30 minutes so all the juices run out. This removes the moisture and concentrates the flavor.

Add 2 tablespoons of the olive oil to a large skillet and panfry each slice of bread until it's golden on both sides, approximately 2 to 3 minutes on each side. Once you remove them from the skillet, sprinkle 1/2 cup of the Parmesan cheese evenly over each slice.

Transfer the tomatoes to a large bowl; then add the remaining 2 tablespoons of olive oil, garlic, the remaining 1/2 cup of Parmesan cheese, red wine vinegar, and basil. Stir gently until well combined.

Evenly spoon the mixture on top of each slice of toast, garnish with a few more leaves of chopped fresh basil and another sprinkle of grated Parmesan cheese, and serve immediately. This recipe is best served fresh. If you make it ahead of time, the tomato mixture or bread can turn mushy. No one wants mushy bruschetta!

"

This magical, marvelous food on our plate,

this sustenance we absorb, has

a story to tell.

It has a journey.

It leaves a footprint.

It leaves a legacy.

—JOEL SALATIN,
FOLKS, THIS AIN'T NORMAL

CHAPTER 6

Food as Gift

In Oak Cliff, an artsy and diverse nook of Dallas, there was a little market called Urban Acres where friends and neighbors gathered around a common interest—local, fresh food. The shelves were filled with Texas produce just pulled from the ground, local milk with cream still on top, eggs and meats from pasture-raised animals, artisan breads baked that morning, and fair-wage coffee roasted down the street.

Urban Acres was our first family business, our first labor of love. Before I became a farmer myself, it was my greatest earthly lesson on the beauty of growing and sharing food.

Steven and I didn't grow up on farms; we grew up in suburbia. We were totally out of our element and didn't really know what to do with strange things like turnips and figs and kombucha. But we were enthusiastic and ready to learn. Perhaps we were also a wee bit crazy and idealistic, but we decided to start a brick-and-mortar business out of this newfound passion. While we consistently peddled farm-fresh goods in a Dallas parking lot every weekend, our co-op grew into the hundreds, and we needed to find a more permanent location, stat. We looked in our own Dallas neighborhood.

To truly envision what Urban Acres was like at the beginning, first picture the neighborhood where it lived—Oak Cliff—which prides itself in being a hidden jewel in the middle of the city. Just over the Trinity River from downtown, Oak Cliff is truly "old Dallas," a historic area where chain stores are few and far between, and mom-and-pop shops and restaurants reign. This neighborhood has it all: steep hills in an otherwise flat city, mature oak trees, authentic taco stands, bike-friendly thoroughfares, prairie- and Craftsman-style houses with wide, inviting front porches, and, heck, even a house on stilts.

In 2010, we opened our first Urban Acres storefront right around the corner from our historic 1940s home in this very neighborhood.

The culture of Urban Acres was birthed from its surroundings and our extremely diverse staff, volunteers, and customers—advocates of authenticity who were as unique as the neighborhood itself. The process through which each farmer's hard-earned golden beets or wild blackberries or baby bellas arrived on someone's dinner table happened because of one word: *community*.

At precisely 11:00 a.m. every Friday, ten of these folks gathered in our warehouse for what we called "the dance." This was when the small team of volunteers, in just a few hours' time, would hand-sort almost *ten thousand pounds* of organic produce into hundreds of individual shares for Dallas families who were members of our produce co-op. Each Friday, it seemed practically impossible. And each Friday, in an impressively orchestrated act of teamwork and camaraderie, they accomplished the impossible with smiles on their faces and high fives all around.

Here's how it worked:

First, the farmers arrived, backing up trucks to the warehouse doors and unloading that week's bounty: baskets overflowing with fresh arugula or bundles of spinach bouquets. Someone pumped up the music, and the sort team would assemble, swigging bottles of water as if in preparation for a marathon: Patrick, Liz, Kathi, Chris, Jamal, Chase, Cynthia, Joe, Jim, Carrie, Saul. The team leader would shout out the first item: "Cauliflower! Two heads in every bin—let's *go*!" The team then scattered and conquered.

Several hours later, the volunteers got to cash in their hours for food credit in our store, which was styled by volunteer Cynthia and decorated with succulents from her backyard repotted into upcycled beer cans and wine bottles. They filled their baskets with fresh produce, gluten-free goodies, farm-fresh dairy, or local honey to take home and enjoy.

Each volunteer had their own reasons for being involved. Some were out of a job and needed food; some had six-figure salaries and just wanted to serve the community; some just thought it was fun. Each of them used their creativity and area of expertise, heading home more connected to the farmers and the land and the people who would eat that fresh food the next day. All those hands working together created something beautiful.

The next morning, we delivered bins full of fresh produce in our refrigerated truck to our "farm stand" pickup locations all over Dallas in churches, nonprofits, or businesses that were already plugged in to their neighborhoods.

Normally, city dwellers hustled around the concrete jungle to make appointments, run errands, and fight traffic. But for a two-hour window at a community garden or in a church parking lot, neighbors gathered and connected as they picked up their shares.

"What's *this*?" a woman would ask, examining the leafy greens resting on top of her bin.

"Oh, that's kale, and I promise if you bake it, it tastes like french fries," another member would respond.

Another question: "Hey, does anyone know what to do with beets?"

"Try roasting them!" someone would pipe up. "It brings out the sweetness."

Conversations flickered and recipes were exchanged, creating an atmosphere reminiscent of the old-time general store but with a lot more skin colors and belief systems.

What we put in the shares each week was a surprise, largely dependent on what was seasonal and available at the time. You should have seen grown men and women hauling bins to their cars and then peeking inside them like kids on Christmas morning.

All the while, I was a young, bleary-eyed first-time mom just trying to be present, help our family business, and keep my own creativity alive.

I worked the register at the store and illustrated chalkboard signs with a newborn baby strapped to my chest. I scrambled to the computer during Luci's nap times to write blog posts for our website, keep up with accounts payable, and file membership forms.

Corresponding with our customers was one of my favorite things: sometimes it meant helping someone figure out how to cook bok choy, and sometimes it meant rescuing them from making a fruit pie out of Swiss chard when they mistook it for rhubarb.

This stage of life was full of delight and also overwhelming; it felt like one of the most challenging things I'd ever done. I felt completely frazzled most days. But it was also the continuation of the simpler, more intentional life we were building around the things that mattered to us.

I remember a particular spring afternoon when I was walking home from our store with a bag of produce on my wrist, a bottle of kombucha in one hand, and my nine-month-old daughter nestled in her carrier against my chest. I saw my reflection in the windows and paused. I saw a glimpse of myself, and I was truly happy with what I saw.

I don't want to forget what it was like then, back at the beginning of this journey that began the Kindred Life.

I don't want to forget seeing someone's eyes light up at the first bite of a Texas blueberry sweeter than candy, especially when I was present when those blueberries were delivered in wooden crates by the farmer who grew them. I don't want to forget the parents and two children who rode their bikes home from our store with produce stuffed into the front baskets. Or the couple who walked home, each holding one side of their produce bin, swinging it between them as if it were a happy toddler.

There's something powerful about food. The abundance of it can cause feelings of thankfulness or, conversely, greed and arrogance. The lack of it can cause humility, or anger and entitlement. Food stirs people emotionally and, ideally, draws us together.

At the heart, our business was about *so much more* than just a head of lettuce or a bunch of kale. I saw miracles grow before me as a single seed that was planted by a farmer on Texas soil ended up having a healing effect on a stranger's life.

At the end of the pickup days, we would drive to South Dallas, randomly knock on people's doors, and see if they wanted some fresh produce. You should have seen their eyes widen—people holding a crate full of lettuce, broccoli, and beets was probably the last thing they were expecting. But it was beyond fulfilling to get more local, farm-fresh food into people's hands, especially in areas where it wasn't readily available.

Once that got to be more than we could personally handle, we partnered with local nonprofits that made sure the food was delivered to people who otherwise wouldn't have access to fresh organic food. We formed relationships with local leaders like Kelly from the 2000 Roses Foundation, who worked with women who were formerly in prison. Or Elizabeth at Promise of Peace Community Garden, who helped get kids off the street by teaching them the value of getting their hands in the dirt. Others delivered to refugees, who had no idea *what* food to buy here in America, much less *where* to buy it.

In 2013, we put our love of sharing meals around the table into action on a bigger scale for our first big farm-to-table dinner, "A Steward's Dinner," at Four Corners Brewing near Oak Cliff. Among the fermenting equipment, we set two long tables for one hundred people down the entire length of the warehouse with mismatched plates, napkins, greenery, and candles. During a keynote by our special guest, Joel Salatin (the man who had inspired us years before to start driving those Texas back roads), we shared a feast and learned what it meant to be stewards of the earth through our food choices.

I honestly don't remember a single thing that was on the menu that night. What I do remember is looking out in awe from the balcony over the twinkle-lit room just before the guests arrived. I remember the many diverse hands, thoughts, and lifestyles—

celebrity chefs working with beekeepers, dairy farmers toasting with lawyers. People who wouldn't normally sit together were breaking bread, sharing common ground.

We knew that evening we were on to something special.

Steven spoke to college classes and news outlets to share with as many people who would listen why local and organic farming is important for our society and our health. We worked in Dallas food deserts by providing farm-fresh food where there wasn't any healthy food available for miles (yes, right under our noses in one of the largest cities in the nation). We even put on a sustainability conference where Joel Salatin returned to break down a butchered pig in front of the entire audience, teaching them how pasture-raised animals contribute to the health of the environment and showing them the contrast of how healthy animals are when they're raised humanely, the way God intended.

Shortly after this first dinner, we launched a Kickstarter campaign so we could expand into a bigger and more functional space. It only seemed fitting that our new place would be crowdfunded by the people who had made it possible. After raising $39,000 through our incredible community (it was the most successful food-related Kickstarter campaign at the time), at the end of 2013 we moved to a larger location in Oak Cliff and built Urban Acres Farmstead, our quarter-acre farm in the city, with chickens, beehives on the roof, rabbits, a hydroponics greenhouse, an organic market and café, and a space for hosting small farm dinners and classes on topics ranging from beginner knife skills to kombucha making.

Our second daughter was born at home just a few days before the ribbon-cutting ceremony for our urban farmstead, but we still attended the celebration—another baby girl strapped to my chest, clinging to a lock of my hair, along for the ride.

Over the next year and a half, we hosted harvest parties, tours of our mini-farm, and granite-stone pizza-oven Friday nights on our patio. We became known for our home-made jumbo cinnamon rolls and Perfect Granola, and as a place where you could slow down and connect to creation, a simpler life, and other people, smack-dab in the middle of the city.

I pushed the double stroller up and down hills on walks to the new farmstead several times a week so my girls could visit Daddy and the chickens and marvel at the cheese counter. We had grown so much in seven years from that first Dallas parking lot and had plentiful stories to tell. We farmed on concrete and lived to tell the tale.

If Urban Acres could have stayed afloat on passion, motivation, idealism, and community, it would still be standing today. The truth is, it takes more than love and passion to run a business that is as successful on paper as it is in lasting, immeasurable ways.

And we learned from our mistakes; we tried to do *everything* rather than just a few things well. For some people, joining a co-op was still a trend and not quite a way of life, and it was common for customers to try it for a few months and then move on to something else. We grew too fast and overcompensated for it. We were doing something really cutting edge in a time when "organic" and "farm to table" were still new in Dallas, and in the end, it just wasn't enough to stay financially profitable.

In early 2015, we knew our time at Urban Acres was waning. Letting go of a company we'd built from scratch and poured everything into for seven years was one of the hardest things we've ever done. Deep down, though, we knew our story was just beginning and that Urban Acres wasn't a failure. We had said yes to a juicier life of risk and change, taking the chance to set out that first cooler of farm-fresh food for people in a Dallas parking lot. We had done our absolute best. What we'd built was more than a business—it was a movement that had made an imprint on the city and people's lives, and they had made an imprint on us, forever.

In the process of selling Urban Acres, we decided to leave Dallas and let go of one dream in order to embrace the possibility of a new one. I'd always wanted to return to Middle Tennessee, where I had gone to college at Belmont University in Nashville. Throughout eleven years in Dallas, I had made the best of city living: nurturing backyard gardens that flourished, uncovering every possible green space, regularly taking my girls on hikes through the forest or nature preserve. Still, I had dreamed of Tennessee's lush, green landscape I'd loved in my college and post-college single days and knew it would call me back one day.

We dared to dream that we could have our own farm now. We had learned enough from our farmer friends to know we wanted to try our hands at being the farmers this time. Tennessee was the only other place in the country where we had actual deep friendships, it was affordable, there was a thriving homeschooling community, and *hello*, it was absolutely beautiful.

It seemed like the perfect place to leap.

We decided to sell our beloved home in Oak Cliff, jam all our stuff into storage, and point our future east on I-30 toward possibility, opportunity, rolling hills, and four distinct seasons.

Because of Urban Acres, we left Texas with a truth firmly planted within us that, turns out, would only strengthen over time.

Food is more than just physical sustenance; it stirs vulnerability, it connects us, it makes us human.

Food is a gift. And I now know the privilege it is to hold that gift in my hands before I pass it along to others.

I'll always be grateful that our family was formed in an environment where everyone was someone. The love of every person from Urban Acres went with us on our new journey. They're just as much a part of our farm today as all the new friends who've gathered around our tables in Tennessee. They're absolutely, undoubtedly part of our kindred.

THIS CHAPTER IS ABOUT

diversity

Food is more than just physical sustenance; it stirs vulnerability, it connects us, it makes us human. Sharing food brings us together in our diversity because it's something we all need and crave. Food is a gift we can hold in our hands and pass along to others to nourish them in all kinds of ways.

- In what ways have you seen that food is more than physical sustenance?

- Have you ever experienced food as a gift—as the giver or the recipient? What was that experience like?

- What's a diverse group of people you've been a part of, and how did a shared food experience play a role in that?

Herb-Roasted Veggies

One benefit of owning an organic produce co-op was that we always had abundant veggies to cook and experiment with at home. Now on the farm, one of our favorite simple dinners is a pan of roasted veggies with creamy dipping sauces, a salad, and some kind of meat: roasted chicken thighs, a whole chicken, sausage, or ground beef. A pan of roasted veggies is quick to prepare, and you can let the veggies roast while you make the rest of your meal.

You want roasted veggies that are perfectly crisp and brown on the outside but soft on the inside. It's an easy set formula you can use with whatever veggies you have on hand.

Here are some of my favorite veggies to roast—any or all of them together: radishes, broccoli, cauliflower, zucchini, yellow squash, potatoes, sweet potatoes, butternut squash, beets, and carrots.

Makes 6 to 8 servings

Approximately 6 cups cubed veggies of choice
2 tablespoons extra virgin olive oil, avocado oil, or coconut oil
1 tablespoon Kindred Farm "The Everyday" Spice Mix

Preheat the oven to 400 degrees.

Peel your veggies as desired, although I recommend leaving the skin on for maximum vitamins! Then cut them into 1-inch pieces.

Fill a roasting pan with the veggies and toss them with the oil and herb blend so all the veggies are coated.

Arrange the veggies in a single layer, leaving space between them. If you crowd the veggies on the pan, they'll steam instead of roast, and you won't get that incredible browning on all sides.

Roast the veggies for 20 minutes. Toss and check them to see if they're becoming golden brown. If not, roast for a few minutes longer.

NOTE
- You can substitute 1 teaspoon salt, 1 teaspoon black pepper, and 1 teaspoon garlic powder for the spice mix.

Herbed Mayo

And because the only thing better than a plate of seasonal roasted veggies is roasted veggies in creamy dipping sauces . . .

Makes 1/2 cup

1/2 cup mayonnaise
1 teaspoon Kindred Farm "The Everyday" Spice Mix, or 1 teaspoon from a mixture
   of equal parts sea salt, black pepper, and garlic powder

In a small mixing bowl, stir the mayo and herb blend together with a spoon until creamy.

I love dipping the roasted veggies into the herb blend—a little creaminess with each bite!

Beet Hummus

Adding a splash of magenta to your plate is unique and fun, and even my girls like this dish because it's bright pink! This hummus would also make for an amazing pop of color on a charcuterie board.

Makes 1 quart

3 to 4 medium beets
1/4 cup tahini
Juice from 1 lemon
1 to 2 cloves garlic
1 to 2 teaspoons cumin
4 tablespoons extra virgin olive oil
Sea salt and cracked black pepper to taste
Optional toppings: drizzle of local raw honey, powdered turmeric, smoked paprika,
   toasted nuts, chopped parsley, or chopped cilantro

Fill a medium-large pot with water. Cut the ends off the beets and place them in the pot. Bring the water to a boil, and boil the beets until fork tender—that is, cooked just enough that a fork passes into the middle of the beet easily.

Drain the beets and let them cool a bit. (If you decide to peel the beets, the skins will slide right off.)

Put the beets in a food processor with the tahini, lemon juice, garlic, and cumin. Pulse until the ingredients start to form a paste.

Using a rubber spatula, scrape the sides of the food processor bowl to make sure all the little bits are in the mixture, and pulse again.

Drizzle in the olive oil a tablespoon at a time, and keep pulsing until the mixture has a creamy consistency.

Add salt and pepper to taste, pulse the mixture again, and sample until you're happy with the level of seasoning.

Scoop the hummus into a small serving bowl and add any optional toppings desired.

NOTES

- You can peel the beets if you like, but you can leave the skins on as well.
- Beet hummus can be stored in a covered container in the fridge for up to one week.

SERVING SUGGESTIONS

- Use the hummus as a dip for raw veggies (carrots, cucumbers, celery).
- Use it as a dip for crackers or chips.
- Spread it on toast and add other toppings, like goat cheese or nuts.
- Use it as a sauce on top of a rice bowl.

"

I'm not a bit changed—not really. I'm only just

pruned down and branched out.

The real me—back here—is just the same.

—L.M. MONTGOMERY,
ANNE OF GREEN GABLES

CHAPTER 7

It's Pronounced "Santa Fee"

I never wanted to leave our house in Dallas—the house where we'd grown love, food, flowers, babies, and friendships. We'd cried many tears there too: through business failures and stresses, broken relationships, and marriage struggles. That home was humble but full of things I loved, like a clawfoot bathtub, ten-foot ceilings, lots of windows, a bright kitchen where we'd cooked a million meals, hallways that had echoed with my girls' giggles—authentic life in all its forms. How could I leave it?

My college roommate and lifelong friend Christy flew in from Nashville to help me. With Ree Drummond whipping up something buttery delicious on TV in the background, I packed our lives away into large brown boxes.

Christy forced me to clean out my kitchen cupboards and put stuff on the curb that didn't need to be carted all the way to Tennessee. Everything else was donated to the Salvation Army or given to friends, like my beloved blue-and-white cruiser bike that Steven had rolled into the room with a giant bow on it at my surprise thirtieth birthday party. It even had a scrolly *S* on the seat for "Stine" (or "Schwinn," *whatever . . .*), symbolizing freedom to me before I'd had children, back when I went on bike rides through the neighborhood without a helmet, the wind whipping through my hair.

I didn't want to let go of that bike, but I gave it to my friend Jessica, knowing she would enjoy it and take care of it. We simply didn't have room in a tiny storage container for things we weren't sure we'd use anytime soon.

Once the packing was finished, we moved out and stayed with friends so we could get some small renovations done. Since we'd just sold Urban Acres, Steven was working seventy hours a week as a consultant for a few restaurants in the area. While writing menus and testing pizza dough recipes, he was also juggling the logistics of talking with the construction workers who were refinishing our floors and painting all my colorful walls a boring shade of Realtor-approved gray.

It wasn't the finest time for our marriage, either. We barely saw each other, and when we did, we only had time to have short, snippy conversations about the house sale or the children before collapsing into bed on an air mattress.

Finally, it came: the breaking point. I caught pneumonia and was sicker than I'd ever been. Months of fighting through trying to save our business, facing the reality that we were selling our home, and all the normal parenting challenges with two small children had caught up with me.

Mercifully, our home sold quickly, and we were able to move on from this weird in-between that was putting so much stress on our family. Our dear friend Michelle came over to take some final photos of us in the backyard . . . the backyard where we'd grown our first tomato.

The girls gathered acorns from under the oak tree Steven and I planted when we first moved in. After snapping one last photo of them running around in circles in their former, empty bedroom with light streaming in the windows, I glanced over my shoulder at the gray walls and realized the house didn't look like my bold, colorful home anymore.

The time had come.

We loaded into our Chevy Tahoe and headed for Tennessee without a job, a place to live, or a plan besides looking for land so we could potentially start our own farm. I was simultaneously excited and completely scared out of my mind—Nashville was the city I loved during college and post college, but it would be different now. With all my might, I clung to the promise that God would go before me,[1] and I even put an image with the verse on my phone lock screen so I would recite it to myself several times a day.

When we first arrived in Tennessee in mid-November, we felt like we'd just arrived at summer camp, fueled by sheer adrenaline and newness. We stayed with a few gracious friends and drove around town all day, following leads and contacts, opening every door to see what might be on the other side. Now that I was here, it felt like my heart was soaring every day with excitement and possibility.

There were so many unknowns, but we saw each day that God really was going before us, several steps ahead, preparing the way.

After a serendipitous encounter with a barista at Muletown Coffee in Columbia, Tennessee, one afternoon, Steven was offered a job as the farm director at Homestead Manor, a forty-acre farm property and event venue. Just days after arriving in Tennessee, he'd been handed the opportunity to farm—without having to spend money yet on our own farm.

Through a series of more miracles, we were then led to kind landlords who had a little rental house on a country road south of Nashville, and we signed a one-year lease.

Within days, we had a home and income.

The weekend we moved in, my dear friend Christy was there again, sleeping on a mattress on the floor, now helping me *unpack* boxes that literally stacked to the top of the vaulted ceiling. The home was basically one giant room, with one bathroom and two bedrooms built off the side, and everything was painted butter yellow.

Even though the style was nothing like what I would have chosen, I was grateful for the provision of the house, remembering what it felt like to pull into Tennessee with nowhere to lay our heads. And the windows! There were nearly panoramic views of the forest behind the house and the steep, cattle-speckled hills across the street.

I concentrated on making it feel like a home while building a new daily life and routines for our little family. It felt strange hanging our pictures on the wall when we had no history in the place, but I was determined that it would feel like "us" for however long we lived there.

Although I had so many dear, close friends in town from when I'd lived there before, and I had also made some new ones, it was difficult starting over in a new place and living in a rural setting for the first time in my life. This social introvert wanted to know:

- How would I fill our days?
- Who would be our everyday people?
- What future were we building here?

Two months in, I hit the wall.

Feeling isolated and regretful, I thought that maybe, just maybe, this whole thing had been a big mistake. I started fantasizing about returning to Texas and wrote detailed plans in my journal about how we could make it happen.

I don't remember exactly what changed my mind to make me feel at home, except that one day, I looked around and realized we had taken "home" with us. There were new pencil marks on my girls' growth chart. There were photos of us in new places, but we were still doing things we loved, like adventuring and exploring and sharing meals with friends. We were in a different state and home, but we were still *us*—the Baileys—just figuring out our way in the world together.

God had *released* us to move, to make a new beginning, but it took me a few months to see it that way. The best gift we'd been given was the gift of time—time to slow down, to carve out space for what matters, and to pay attention to the everyday treasures.

For the first time in years, we didn't own a home or a business, and all our belongings fit in a tiny storage shed in the yard. I'd always seen it as a gift (and my choice) to be able to be home with my daughters. Now I realized the difference in *being truly present* versus just *being around*. After years of fighting fiercely through financial and personal struggles, we could simply abide.

With this renewed perspective, I was finally able to release all the pent-up emotions of the last many months of intense transition. The gift had been in front of me the entire time since we'd moved, but I hadn't seen it. Now I couldn't unsee it.

Our year in the rental house was a season of abundance that wasn't about money or things but gifts much more difficult to measure. We explored our yard and drove the rolling hills. We homeschooled and flew kites. We drew and played pretend. I learned how to make bread for the first time in my life, and after I'd practiced doing so many times, Chef Steven declared it "baller." We were in closer quarters than ever before and learned to make daily sacrifices to live on a cash system, to figure out how to feed our family healthy food when we no longer owned a produce co-op, and to say no to unnecessary things so we could say yes to the ultimate life we wanted.

That little home surrounded by stunning woods and meadows will always be where Norah was two years old and spirited and hilarious. That home will always be where Luci was five—going on six—and a bigger little girl every day. There will always be a spot on the kitchen floor where they loved to show me their made-up dances to vintage Disney songs on the record player.

It'll always be where I heard and saw their imaginations take flight—playing family or restaurant or making a fort and café in the closet.

The transition was hard, but the release brought peace and the gift of a fresh perspective—a perspective that was essential to helping prepare me for what was coming next.

⌒—⁓

In August 2016, I found myself standing on the pavement in the middle of Central Park in New York City, sweating bullets.

We'd decided to take a break from the Tennessee humidity to visit my parents in New Jersey as well as Steven's sister, Michelle, and her family, who had just moved to Queens, New York. Instead, we exchanged Tennessee humidity for a northeastern heat wave; it was over one hundred degrees as we walked through Central Park. We drenched our shirts and shorts and begged for another five-dollar bottle of water from the man pulling a cooler on wheels.

After a few scorching days in the city, we escaped the hustle and bustle to take a thirty-mile drive to Stone Barns Center for Food and Agriculture. Stone Barns is a gorgeous eighty-acre farm on land donated by the Rockefellers that educates new farmers and the public on regenerative agriculture through innovative farming practices. It's also the home of Chef Dan Barber's renowned farm-to-table restaurant, Blue Hill, with a menu built around food grown on the farm.

The place was enchanting in the most rustic, serene, simple way. The entire visit was a deep exhale, from the moment we pulled into the winding driveway lined with green pastures where chickens and sheep grazed and bee colonies thrived. Even in the intense heat, we walked around freely, our girls skipping beside us through the stone and wood buildings to go see what was growing in the fields and greenhouses. In the on-site café, we sampled delectable baked goods, quiches, and salads all made and grown at Stone Barns, eating every last bite while sitting on a bench in the wildflower and herb garden with bees and butterflies swarming around us.

As I weaved in and out of the sunflowers, entranced, pausing to study giant bumble bees gorging themselves on pollen, I knew deep in my bones that my hands were made for growing, for creating tangible beauty in some way like this.

The next week, I wrote these lines in my journal:

> Something stirred deep within me at Stone Barns last week . . . can't stop thinking about it. Maybe it's that our vision as a family is basically a mini version of that place. Maybe it was the wildflower garden and longing to get my hands in the soil again and grow something and take more ownership over my life. I'm actively seeking what this stirring is, and I'm sure more of the journey will be revealed soon.

After that trip to the northeast, Steven and I started getting antsy. We were willing to stay another year in our rental house but couldn't help the feeling that it was time to (literally) put our hands to the plow again. It felt strange not to be doing hard work together, working toward a cause. And although we were buying food from the farmers market, I deeply missed growing our own produce and cooking with it.

I still wasn't sold on the whole *living on a farm* thing yet; the idea sounded lovely in a "farfetched dream" kind of way. It sounded like it would be nice to have acres of land to call our own, but I was afraid I'd left behind a life I loved for a new life I wasn't sure I'd be able to love. It felt safer to keep it a daydream.

As our lease was coming to an end, we started casually searching online for properties in the area, but everything we found in our price range was either (a) blank land with no house on it, or (b) beautiful land with a really rundown fixer-upper house.

I mean, I had my limits. There was no way this girl was signing up for building *both* a farm *and* a home from scratch. All we needed was some good open land that wasn't too hilly or forested and an unfancy house that was niceish and move-in ready. We kept looking.

One day, in the fall of 2016, a photo of a small, olive-green farmhouse popped up on the realty website.

It was in Santa Fe, Tennessee. Wherever that was.

"Wait . . . I haven't seen this one before. It must be new," I said to Steven.

The photos of the inside of the home reminded me of our Dallas house—it was Craftsman style, built in a similar time period. There were seventeen acres of land, twelve of which were open pasture. It had definite potential.

We drove down I-65 out of Nashville, past the malls and chain stores into the rolling green countryside. When we arrived in Santa Fe, I plastered my face to the window, taking in the impossibly gorgeous views—cottages and farmhouses, silos, autumn leaves falling like confetti over rolling hills dotted with wildflowers, sheep, and cows. The scenes were like real-life paintings from my childhood storybooks, the ones with the worn spines that my mom had read over and over at bedtime.

We pulled in the gravel driveway of the green farmhouse with a huge field of blank, unkempt land behind it. The current owners had been moved out for a while, and the real estate agent said we were allowed to look around. As we got out of the car, my red Salt Water sandals stepped onto the land, sinking deeply into the thick, cushy grass.

And I *knew*.

As difficult as it can be for me to make decisions, there are a few times in my life when I've just known right away, like when I realized "that guy in Dallas" was going to be my husband.

Maybe because my heart was already fertile ground from the year we'd just spent abiding, I felt a kinship with the land immediately. I knew this soil was where we would continue our journey of growing food, family, and community.

I opened the front door with the original 1940s skeleton key and slowly walked in the living room, looking around at the hardwood floors and the historic details. "This place feels like us."

In the master bathroom, I found a vintage clawfoot soaking tub, and my girls actually started cheering. Minus the fact that the rooms were cave-like with every single wall painted dark-chocolate brown, the layout and character were so similar to our old, beloved house.

Exploring the yard, the girls ran through a wide, grassy corridor bordered by pine trees on one side and a small creek on the other and immediately started collecting pine cones.

We didn't know it yet, but the space they were playing in would shortly become known as "the Forest of Fun," with well-loved swings hanging from the trees. A few years later, its length and width and level ground would be perfect for long, white-dressed farm tables set end-to-end, filled with people clinking glasses, slowing down, savoring the fruits of the land for our first summer Kindred Dinner.

The farmhouse would soon be christened with drawings of giraffes and mermaids and unicorns on the refrigerator, scuffs on the walls from our girls' crazy antics, and measurements of their growth on the dining room door frame.

We moved in on a bright December day, filling another home with our belongings and personality.

The transition was rough at first. Here I was, finally on our own land, and I panicked.

I sat on the front porch, staring at the empty fifty-miles-per-hour road outside our front door, pining away so much for the walks we used to take around our old neighborhood in Dallas that my stomach twisted with a pang of sadness for the life we'd left behind. I couldn't fully let go of the past—the place my babies were born, where they took their first steps, and where Steven and I became a family.

While we'd talked for years about having our farm one day, it was easier to dismiss the fears of change and the unknowns of living in the country when we were in a temporary situation. This was more permanent—we had literally *bought the farm.*

And we didn't even know how to pronounce the name of our new town correctly. We were graciously informed by locals that it's pronounced "Santa Fee," *not* like Santa Fe, New Mexico, so we didn't make fools of ourselves at the post office.

At the core of my concerns was a fear of disconnection, of remoteness living in the country, and ultimately, of distance from people. Santa Fe— or *"Santa Fee"* or whatever—was a good thirty minutes *farther* away from town than the rental house we'd just left. Our oldest daughter

was six, and our youngest was three, and playdates with friends we'd worked so hard to find in a new city were now weekly staples.

Although in my heart of hearts I knew I was made for living in a place with more green and space and freedom, I resisted it at first, thinking I wasn't really cut out for living in a rural setting.

Would we be isolated here?

Would anyone ever come to our house?

Would we have a close community again?

Where would my kids learn to ride a bike?

What would we do without sidewalks?

I wish I could say my fears were all magically fixed, but a feeling of being settled took effort, time, and trust in the goodness of the journey we were on.

With little flickers of bravery here and there, I started to see that connection—to people, to the land, and to a new life full of purpose—was closer than I thought.

By taking one more step forward and then another, I began to uncover the unexpected gifts—glimmering, small treasures—waiting on the other side.

First, there were the discoveries on our land. After nine years of living in an urban neighborhood with two trees in our front yard and zero in the backyard, we now had a towering wild persimmon tree full of edible fruit, an apple tree, and five acres of forest filled with more trees than we could imagine. Some of their trunks were five feet wide, and their limbs stretched to the heavens.

There was a long, rectangular cedar cabin in the woods full of random items left behind by previous owners, and the first time we dug through it, we found not only a plethora of mouse hotels but also vintage tin tea kettles, tools, chess and checkers games, loads of spray paint, lanterns, bean bags, and street signs.

And then, a real treasure. While poking around in the woods behind the cabin one day, I saw a flash of something blue partially covered in dead leaves, leaning against a tree. I walked through the woods closer to it, pushing aside branches that scratched my cheeks and clothes.

It was a blue-and-white Schwinn cruiser bike—*exactly* like the beloved one I had left behind in Dallas, all the way down to the color and "S" on the seat.

The tires were flat and the handlebars rusty, but other than that, it was in pretty good condition, like it had barely been ridden. I mean, what on earth? Why was this bike here? *What are the chances?*

Speechless and incredulous, I clutched the handlebars, realizing I held in my hands a tangible, unexplainable demonstration of God's love for me. I got it out of the woods immediately, zip-tied an old wire shopping basket from Urban Acres to the handlebars, and leaned it against the side of the other smaller cedar cabin next to our house that would eventually become our farm store. With its basket filled with flowers in every season, it would be a permanent fixture and daily reminder of God's provision, kindness, and attention to detail.

Surprises kept coming that first bleak winter. One night shortly after we moved in, we were cranking out some homemade pasta with friends with the back door open. Suddenly, I felt something weaving in and out of my ankles. "Um, does anyone know where this cat came from?" Enter Ginger the Adventure Cat, our farm cat who adopted us and hasn't left to this day.

In February, the sky-scraping loblolly pines out the dining room window saved my life when there was nothing else green and all I could think about was the lushness and possibility of springtime. I found that the front porch in the morning was a great place to take my first sip of hot coffee while Snow Creek constantly rushed across the street on our neighbor's property. I discovered that our own little seasonal creek, which our girls named Fairy Creek, only flowed when it rained, and fairies left behind bits of moss and tiny pebbles.

Our first spring, with lemongrass tea in hand and Ginger purring against my legs, I giddily investigated the blooming things in our yard. Bright-yellow forsythia, the epitome of happiness, was the first flower to open her petals, which immediately took me back to my childhood backyard in New Jersey. After that was a daily symphony, a new flower seemingly unfolding every day: redbuds, violas, plum, wisteria, buttercups, daffodils, dogwoods, white lilacs that smelled like the ones my mom grew, and four giant bushes of peonies. The apple tree bloomed and buzzed as one giant, alive being, its branches teeming with bees excitedly gathering pollen from flowers that smelled like heaven.

And then, there were the people who came out of the woodwork. Remember those fears about being isolated? It didn't take long to realize that people here (a) often stop by unannounced and (b) are more happily available.

One evening, I sent a batch of my husband's homemade kimchi, a steaming hot loaf of bread, and some essential oils home with a neighbor, Sarah, whose daughter had just injured her finger in a car door. Sarah, her husband, and their two kids live a few miles down the road. Funny enough, Santa Fe's barely-there internet connection is what first connected us, and the first time we met, we made friends easily, chattering on about homemade kimchi, backyard chickens, herb gardens, and DIY home design. When Sarah arrived at the door that evening to retrieve the essential oils I'd offered them, she handed me a jar of herbs and wildflowers from her garden. I froze for a moment because I was honestly caught off guard to receive a gift when *she* was the one with the hurt child at home. But that's just the way things are here.

Another day, a family with teenagers whose land borders ours showed up on our doorstep to introduce themselves. In the city, we'd never had neighbors come to our door before "just to visit," but it felt like a hearkening back to the way things used to be and how they should still be. We've since become good friends with those neighbors, sharing a pot of morning coffee or sending goodies back and forth on paper plates. We let them borrow our farm equipment, and they help us with our bee colonies. They deliver s'mores bars or homemade venison sausage to our front door. We deck their dinner table with fresh flowers.

One stormy afternoon, a neighbor we hadn't met before knocked on the door to let us know that four colossal pigs had escaped and were crossing the road in front of our house. "Are they yours?" They were. He'd already rounded them up, by the way, and they were standing at the back door, staring sheepishly up at me.

Sweet Virginia down the road hand delivers a tin of homemade fudge and baked goods at Christmastime. When he was alive, Mr. Garry would beep and wave every time he drove past our farmhouse in his 1950 Chevy truck and pull in the driveway so our kids could sit on its worn velvet seats. Jim and Sandy across the street have so graciously offered for us to play in their magical stretch of Snow Creek whenever we want without asking, and they really mean it. They recently paved their long, winding driveway along the creek and invited my girls to *ride bikes* on it. Seriously? I didn't see that one coming.

This community is different from a big city, and while our multiracial family misses the cultural diversity, there's definitely diversity: a ukulele-playing grandpa, a weaver, photographers of all different styles, an architect, a chef, a farmer who also works for an African women's health organization, woodworkers, mule trainers, musicians, baristas, and artists. These folks with all different talents and passions also have diverse spiritual and political perspectives, family backgrounds, and life stories that make our community richer.

Perhaps it's partly the novelty of farm life, but we've had more people of all ages visiting us since we moved to the farm than we *ever* did in a city of 1.3 million people. Our guest room has been a revolving door of friends old and new who are desperate for quiet and space and want to get their hands dirty too. And honestly, the one bar of cell phone reception and our extremely weak internet connection have kinda been a blessing—people who come here really don't have any other choice but to put down their phones.

Hospitality and gathering people around the table is as important to us as it was before, only magnified. Now we get to host large groups of people at our seasonal Kindred Dinners and connect with smaller groups of neighbors and customers every Saturday morning at our farm store. Several times a month, we invite old and new friends over to have a Korean food feast, hike around our land, or spend hours around a campfire in the backyard with nowhere to be, drinking wine while our kids play nearby.

Five years later? I've found that by facing my fears about living in the country, I've stepped into a life that is the complete opposite of my fears.

One of the hardest and most important truths I've learned on the farm is that sometimes you have to cut down something that's still growing in order to make room for something new. A new, fresh crop that goes with the season.

What looks like loss is often life actually making room for something better—*more* freedom, *more* growth, *more* fullness. But first, we have to be uprooted.

Trust the uprooting.

I know it's scary, but we can be afraid and still be brave. We must trust that God is for us, and he will go before us.

We can't let fear stop us from doing the actions that bring us one step closer to the life we're meant to live.

So send the email.

Start creating.

Pursue the opportunity.

Leave something behind that isn't working.

Dare to set foot on the new soil.

You don't have to pack up everything and move to the country, I promise! You have your own song, remember? We're not all meant to live on farms, but we are all meant to live slower, richer, more nourishing lives of connection, surrounded by community, *wherever* we are.

In the end, the choices that matter most are those that drive us closer into authentic relationship with people. The family, the cobbled together group of friends who feels like family, the village. Your people. Your kindred. This is how we were created to abide.

Things will be different after this, but don't worry. The authentic parts of you won't be lost; they'll go with you. You'll find your blue cruiser bike waiting for you around that clearing in the trees, just on the other side of change.

THIS CHAPTER IS ABOUT

change

Sometimes you have to cut down something that's still growing in order to make room for something new. A new, fresh crop that goes with the season.

- Let's think about change—the good kind, the kind that moves you forward. Are you being "uprooted" right now in any way?

- Is there something in your life that looks like loss but could instead be making way for a new, better "crop" to grow in this season?

- What are you afraid of losing if you change?

- How is fear stopping you from doing the actions that bring you closer to the life you want to live?

- What are some things you're stirred to do now—big or small—to move in the direction of good, healthy change?

Easiest Bread Recipe Ever

During our time at the rental house after we moved to Tennessee, I started making this bread. It was the perfect recipe to work on during our "abiding" year, and now I've made it at least a hundred times since we moved to the farm. If you come to my house for dinner, I'll likely make you this bread.

There's something about handing someone a warm loaf of bread that makes them feel special and cared for. It's my favorite thing to deliver to foster care families at our church or any friend who's just had a baby. I wrap the bread, still warm, in parchment paper and deliver it with a chicken or pasta dish with tomato sauce, a big Kindred Farm salad, and brownies.

This crusty bread with a lush, soft inside goes perfectly with pretty much anything, from a steaming hot bowl of soup on a chill-you-to-your-bones winter day to a tangy, crunchy salad in early spring (so you can sop up all the extra dressing on your plate with the bread, of course).

Making homemade bread always seemed so complicated and unattainable, but once I finally mustered up the courage to try it, I realized how easy it is. With only a few ingredients, you can whip up the dough in three minutes, then go enjoy the most heavenly scent ever wafting through your house. In the words of my oldest daughter, "I wish they made an essential oil of the baking bread smell!" Me too, sister, me too.

Yes, it's a little more work than buying bread at the grocery store, but do you want to be a part of actual, real magic? Because that's what happens when you make your own bread. With the added ingredient of time, you completely transform a pile of the simplest of ingredients—flour, water, yeast, and salt—into the ultimate hearty comfort food. Baking bread is a slow, intentional practice as ancient as humanity itself, and you get to take part in that when you sink your fingers into that dough.

You can do this—I promise! All you need is a Dutch oven or other tightly lidded pot. I use an inexpensive 5-quart Lodge cast-iron Dutch oven for mine, and I love it.

Makes 1 loaf (6 to 8 servings)

3 cups organic all-purpose flour, plus more for dusting

1 teaspoon active dry yeast from a packet

2 teaspoons sea salt or kosher salt

1 1/2 cups warm water (not hot, which can kill the yeast)

2 tablespoons chopped fresh herbs, like rosemary and thyme, optional

Measure each cup of flour by filling the cup to overflowing, then tap the flour mound with the blade of a butter knife to eliminate any air bubbles and make sure the flour settles into the cup. Use the butter knife to scrape the excess flour off the top of the cup in a straight line. Add each cup of flour to a large bowl, then add the yeast and sea salt.

Add the warm water to the dry mixture and stir it together with a wooden spoon, scraping the sides of the bowl. (The mixture will be sticky and shaggy—that's how it's supposed to look!)

Cover the bowl tightly with plastic wrap and let the dough rise for 6 to 8 hours. Letting it rise on your kitchen countertop is fine, or you can put the bowl in the middle rack of your turned-off oven, with just the oven light on. The warmth from the oven light will help it rise. After the first rise, your dough should have doubled in size and have lots of bubbles.

Preheat the oven to 450 degrees. Place your Dutch oven or lidded oven-safe pot in the oven to get it nice and hot.

While the pot heats, complete the second dough rise. Take a handful of flour and sprinkle it on a cutting board so your dough doesn't stick. Scrape all the dough from the bowl onto the board. (Keep the bowl—you'll need it again!) The dough will be sticky. Sprinkle flour on top, take a flap of dough, and fold it over itself, almost like you're closing an envelope. Keep rotating it and folding it over itself, sprinkling more flour as needed. Your dough should feel soft and puffy and no longer sticky. Turn the dough over, and you'll have a lovely ball with all folds hidden underneath.

Place a piece of parchment paper inside the bowl that previously held the dough. Set your dough ball on the parchment paper in the bowl. Cover the bowl lightly with a clean dish towel, not touching the dough.

Wait about 30 minutes, and you're ready to bake! Open the oven and carefully remove the superhot lid of your Dutch oven. Pick up the parchment paper with the dough ball in it and place the entire thing in the Dutch oven. This way, you won't mess up that perfectly round ball!

Place the lid back on the pot. It's okay if some of the parchment paper sticks out. Bake for 30 minutes. Remove the lid and bake for 15 more minutes, until there's a gorgeous, dark-brown crust. Take the Dutch oven out of the oven. Remove the bread from the Dutch oven and let it cool for a few minutes on a cutting board before slicing.

Give yourself a high five for making homemade bread!

NOTES

- For really crispy crust, use bread flour. My favorite brand is King Arthur.
- I prefer using active dry yeast from packets—not from a jar, which has an extra additive.
- I'll often make this dough right before bed and let it rise overnight, then bake it first thing in the morning. Or I'll make the dough in the morning and let it rise all day so I can bake it before dinner.

Whipped Honey Butter

Out of all the things we serve at our Kindred Dinners, it's the Whipped Honey Butter that people always beg to take home with them. People have even asked for a spoon to eat it straight out of the jar. For our dinners, we partner with a local baker to make the bread since we need such a large quantity, and we serve it with this butter.

Put this butter in a cute jar and take it as a gift to someone, along with the above bread, or have this at the table for everyone to share with their bread at dinner.

It's super simple, but the quality of the butter, the local raw honey, and the amount of time you whip it are all keys to making this the most velvety, ridiculously amazing thing you can slather on your bread.

Makes approximately 1 pint

2 sticks grass-fed butter, softened
1/2 cup local raw honey, plus more to taste
1/4 teaspoon sea salt

In a food processor or stand-up mixer, combine the butter, honey, and salt. You could also use a large bowl and an electric handheld mixer.

Whip/process the butter for several minutes, until it looks light and fluffy like buttercream icing.

Stop and taste. Keep drizzling in more honey and tasting it until you no longer say, "It still tastes like butter," and you can finally say, "Ahh, it tastes like honey butter."

"

If you are lucky enough to find

a way of life you love,

you have to find the courage to *live* it.

—JOHN IRVING,
A PRAYER FOR OWEN MEANY

CHAPTER 8

Progress over Perfection

O n the first day of spring 2017, exactly ten years from when we started our first postage stamp–size garden in Dallas, a large tractor broke ground in the empty field ten steps outside our back door, plowing up the soil of what would become Kindred Farm. Seventeen acres of neglected land, full of hope and possibility. Another chance to begin again, another new piece of paper.

I chose the name *Kindred* for our farm because I've been a writer and lover of words as long as I can remember, and it's always been one of my favorite words. It means "tribe" or "family." In the seventeen years Steven and I have been together, from our little Dallas condo under a highway overpass to our beloved home of nine years in an urban neighborhood to our farmhouse now in the hills of Tennessee, we've been people gatherers; it's part of the DNA of our marriage. The name perfectly embodied where we came from and what we were intentional about building in the city—a life of connection, not waiting for someday.

We had big plans for hosting people here on this land—friends around the table and campfire, farm dinners in the field with produce we had actually grown—and it was going to take a lot of work. I was fueled by the vision of "kindred" and how I wanted people to feel when they set foot here: more connected to their Creator, to their true selves, to the land, and to one another.

There was only one wee little problem. I hadn't actually farmed a day in my life.

Sure, I'd grown plenty of food in our Texas backyard gardens, but that space equaled *one tiny corner* of the field of plowed dirt that was now staring back at me from the other side of my kitchen window. Steven had much more farming experience, but neither of us had done this on our own huge, positively blank piece of Tennessee soil.

While being mentored by a seasoned farmer, Ben, whom we'd met at a farmers market the previous year, our plan was to raise pigs for pork, raise chickens for eggs, and grow produce using sustainable farming methods following the "market gardener" model. Instead of large tractors and other machinery, we would use a walk-behind tractor and manual hand tools to keep our farm small scale and manageable. We would grow as much and as big a variety of produce as possible on less than an acre and sell it at local farmers markets.

Since we were just beginning, we weren't sure what direction this was all going. We just knew we had to begin and see what unfolded. In true "Team Bails" style, we figured it out together, one little step at a time.

The heritage-breed piglets we'd ordered would be arriving soon, so the first thing we did was start setting up the animal pastures. On a chilly Saturday, our entire family of four, including a very enthusiastic toddler, puttered around the farm for hours in our vintage '86 Ford F-150 farm truck (named Hurley), setting up posts and electrical wire and carving out paddocks for the pastures where the chickens and pigs would roam. I'll never forget that day because it'll forever be the day I learned that a "pile driver" is *not* just a term for the crazy WWE wrestling moves my older brother used to practice on me

as a kid. It's actually a tool to drive T-posts into the ground, and it makes your biceps hurt like hell.

Next, we picked up a shipment of fuzzy, adorable chicks in a loudly chirping box at our rural post office—Rhode Island Reds, Araucanas, and Barred Rocks who would, in a few months, become our pastured chicken flock. For their future home, we bought an old chicken trailer that already had roosts and nesting boxes so we could easily move them from pasture to pasture every few weeks. We'd learned from people like Joel Salatin and all our Texas farmer friends that this was the best way to keep the land flourishing and the animals healthily grazing and eating grass and bugs the way they were meant to. We christened it the "Henstream."

And then it was go time: the seedlings we'd started were ready to be planted in the field.

I showed up on day one of spring planting in my new, shiny Ariat work boots with literally no clue what to do next. I didn't know how irrigation lines worked, how deeply to plant the seedlings, how to use a broad fork, how to hook up irrigation, how to cut the "suckers" off tomatoes (or even what a "sucker" was), or how to correctly pick up a chicken.

It was baptism by fire out there.

That day, with our two girls by our sides the entire time, Steven and I prepped and planted our first hundred-foot cabbage row.

First, I learned to use the broad fork, which is basically a giant fork you stand on and pull back to loosen, lift, and aerate the soil. While I can now broad fork an entire row in thirty minutes, that first row took me *two solid hours*, and I could barely walk afterward.

This was just the first of the many uncomfortable feelings I'd have to welcome and embrace if I wanted to grow anything.

Next, we shoveled multiple loads of compost into the dump cart of our tractor to spread down the row and hauled bags of pelleted chicken fertilizer. Steven spread it all out with the harrow, and then it was time to lay the irrigation drip lines, stake down the landscape fabric, and finally, plant the cabbage seedlings. We pushed through the sweat and exhaustion and laid that first row of cabbage together, as a family. And it felt victorious! Afterward, I took a panoramic photo from the upstairs bathroom window, and we celebrated.

During that first season of building the farm from scratch, we started using the phrase "progress over perfection." This is a saying we now have that's as common as breathing.

"Progress over perfection" reminds us that we are capable of changing and growing—and that there is so much completely and beautifully out of our control.

Perfection isn't even possible. If we get hung up on perfection in farming, we'll fail almost every time because we're dealing with nature. Seeds get killed by a late frost. Irrigation lines bust and leak. But progress works; we keep moving forward, learning from our mistakes, and getting better at what we do. And that's what we kept in mind as we fumbled through the rest of that first farming season.

There were baskets of abundant veggies, buckets of sweat, a few tears, sore muscles, and a whole lot of hilarious blunders.

One day, Steven handed me a bag of cover crop seeds, a seeding bag where you pour the seeds to scatter them onto the soil by turning a crank, and an instruction manual. "Go seed the back of the field," he said. "It'll be easy!"

I briefly scanned the instructions, strapped on the bag, and headed for the field, perhaps a little overconfidently. *I mean, how hard could this be?*

I started walking down the row while turning the crank to release seeds. And that's when *all* the seeds—*thousands*—dumped out in one spot at my feet. I was mortified. For the next few months, you could spot our farm from miles away by looking for the world's biggest mound of clover in the back of the produce field.

Once the chicks were old enough, we moved them out of their temporary spot into the Henstream. Steven handed me each pullet one by one as they squawked and rained feathers down on my ponytail. But we got them all safely in there—phew.

That evening, Steven was gone cooking for one of his clients, so I was in charge of checking on the feathered girls at dusk to make sure they all made it inside the automatic chicken door for the night.

No big deal; I strutted out there. At first glance, all looked fine. Then a lone chicken roaming around caught my eye. I chased it around until I finally caught it, took a deep breath, wrangled the door open with one hand, squealed like a twelve-year-old girl, and shoved the chicken inside as it squawked. But it wasn't over yet. As I was leaving, I noticed something looked strange at the chicken door. *Oh no . . . is it? It couldn't be.* Yes, there was a chicken head/neck hanging completely limp out the chicken door while the rest of its body was inside. I frantically called Steven and told him that one of our chickens got decapitated and it was all my fault. I told him that *he* was going to handle it when he got home.

An hour later, he went to take care of the dead chicken and came back inside laughing. "Um, it wasn't dead! It was just frozen in shock. I opened the door and nudged it a little, and it popped its head up and walked away."

In early April, we got six Berkshire black heritage piglets from Farmer Johnny at Taylor Family Farms. Because we didn't even have a barn yet, we nestled them safely into an area we'd prepared in our neighbor's barn to train them on the electric fence before we set them to pasture. Steven and I filled up their food and water and closed the gate, super proud of ourselves.

Thirty seconds later, after high-fiving and exchanging some pleasantries about how surprisingly smoothly the whole thing had gone, we looked at the pig pen, and it was completely empty.

Sure enough, all six of those naughty little piglets had somehow busted out of the barn and were off on their own pigventures, our hard-earned money gallivanting through the woods on six sets of tiny hooves.

Lord, have mercy. What could we do but go after them? Our ever-loyal friend Joe, who was visiting from Dallas and happened to be dressed in shiny Lululemon slacks

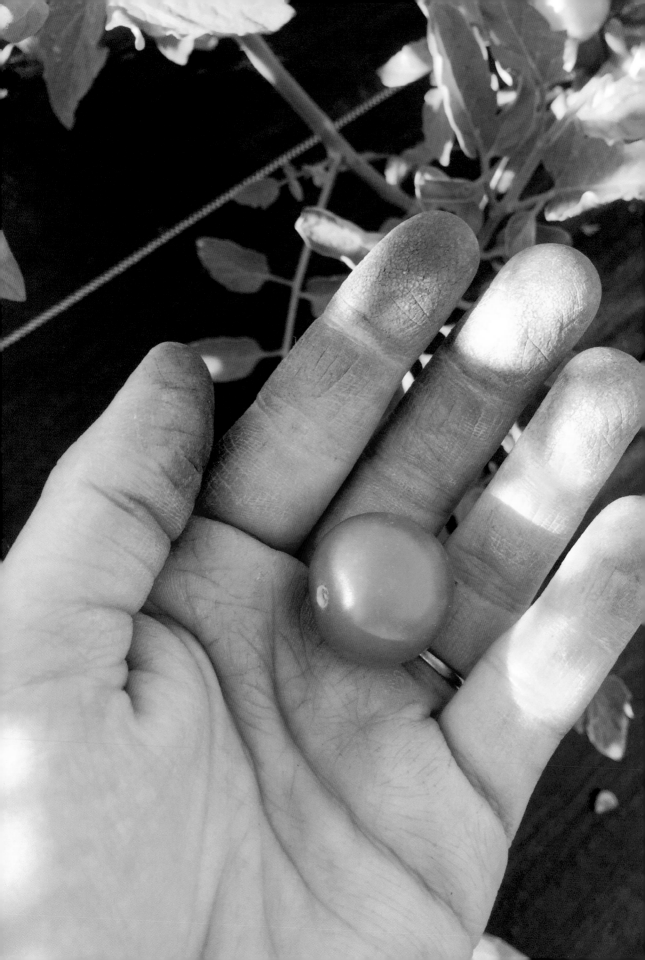

and a button-down, chased them through the woods with us. It took Steven, Joe and his wife, Kathe, the entire family of neighbors living next door (including a grown man and three strapping teenage boys), and me to get those mischievous piglets back in the barn.

The ups and downs of farm life were emotionally taxing. With all the beauty we were building, it seemed that every day, something went completely, horribly wrong: irrigation lines busted, animals went missing, or we were broadsided in some way. Every morning, I woke up unsure if I was going to be fixing something, laughing hysterically, mourning, or rejoicing.

A few weeks later, on a perfect spring day when the piglets were finally ready to be moved to pasture, Ginger the Adventure Cat birthed five kittens. That particular day, it felt like nothing could go wrong with the world: chickens and pigs were grazing happily, daisies and blackberries were growing wildly, and kittens were mewing on the front porch adorably.

And then? *Boom.* Four of Ginger's precious kittens were lost to a predator in the night. Ginger showed up at our back door with the remaining kitten in her mouth, and we were devastated, hit with the terrible, harsh reality of farm life: there will be life, and there will also be death.

Progress over perfection.

I was quickly learning, much to my chagrin, just how far from perfect this messy life was. I still moved forward, choosing to love the thriving and growing life we had, but perhaps with looser hands.

By May, we were up while the moon was still glowing bright to harvest buckets and armfuls of kale and bright, happy stalks of rainbow chard for the farmers market. And we honestly couldn't believe that just five months earlier, there was no farm, just a big field behind our house with a few old, abandoned chicken coops and tall grass.

By June, I held the first ripe red cherry tomato in my tarred hands. It felt so precious that it might as well have been a ruby. And then the first egg from our chickens—a light-blue Araucana egg that exactly matched the wall color in our dining room.

By July, during a humid afternoon pruning two hundred feet of tomatoes, I was overcome by a distinctly earthy and grassy smell and the feel of the tomato tar on my hands. I suddenly channeled the strength of my Italian immigrant grandfather, Stefano, who turned his entire backyard into a tomato garden. I realized for the first time that this was familiar. This was in my blood.

By August, we were barely standing, doing the bare minimum it took to keep things alive in the scorching heat and unrelenting humidity. I had been schooled by the farm many times over. The bug bites, the ticks, the weeds—it was all so much. But the pastures where the chickens and pigs had been grazing were flourishing, and the greenest-of-green grass sprouted up boldly. The land was being healed, regenerated.

By October, we finally saw some relief. While we would continue growing in our new high-tunnel hoop house all winter, most of the field was covered cozily under tarps. Our very rustic yet sturdy barn was also completed. We scratched "KINDRED" in the concrete and stamped our little girls' handprints next to it.

At the end of 2017, our first farming season, I was scarred and shell-shocked for sure. But I was also filled to the brim.

With a whole lot of grit, determination, and hard work, we'd built infrastructure, plowed, sowed, planted, and grown food to share with hundreds of people. We'd grown probably forty varieties of produce—cabbage *way* bigger than our heads, multitudes of peppers, herbs, gorgeous broccoli and spinach bouquets, rows of lettuce that looked like carpets of giant green and purple roses, pink oyster mushrooms that fluttered like ruffles on a little girl's dress.

I thought about the thousands of pounds of produce our little plot of land had yielded for the community. Each seedling we'd grown had a miraculous story—a seed no bigger than a fingernail had grown to become a meal on someone's dinner table, perhaps for a special party or celebration or a child's first time tasting a tomato.

We had no way of knowing where each carefully tended plant had ended end up; we'd just done our part to nourish the soil, grow, and send them out into the world.

But the biggest surprise? It was the transformation inside me. I wasn't just married to a farmer; I *was* a farmer now.

I knew I could nourish the land, but I had no idea that a terrain could nourish *me* emotionally and spiritually. Getting deep in the dirty mess to cultivate beauty felt right. So right.

I'd wasted so much time on fears and worries: *Am I actually cut out for this? Can I really live on a farm with all its challenges and struggles?* Instead of losing myself, I'd found myself. Farming was pushing me physically and emotionally and helping me see what I was truly capable of as a woman—a woman who was much stronger than she'd ever realized.

I slipped on my leather farm boots and realized I was walking differently in the world, with more authority, more agency. A few months—but seemingly a lifetime—removed from that groundbreaking day in the spring, I looked down at the creases in my boots, the caked dirt, the scuffs, the worn soles. And I knew I'd earned every single one of them— from being strong, brave, and willing to walk into the unknown.

Progress over perfection.

Maybe you, like me, have spent a lot of your life working hard to achieve and maintain perfection.

If I've learned anything since becoming a farmer, it's that striving for perfection is absolutely paralyzing.

Perfection idealizes what we hope the end result will be—the dream home, family, career, marriage, friendship—while failing to see the nitty-gritty beauty along the muddy way.

Progress, on the other hand, says that abundant life isn't found in the end result but in the journey itself. Progress says we can't wait to be freed from our fears before moving forward because it's in *walking through them* that we are actually freed. When we're connected to the Creator, each forward motion helps us become more deeply rooted in our unique purpose.

Despite the imperfections, mistakes, and blunders, I truly believe that choosing to cultivate beauty and connection on this earth—with people, the land, and our God-given selves—will never be wasted. It will always be a good investment.

And when we take time to stop and pause and see how far we've come, what we'll be proud of is how we walked through life in the messy middle, when our muscles ached and trembled and we felt like quitting but we chose to continue putting one foot in front of the other.

THIS CHAPTER IS ABOUT

growth

Perfection idealizes what we hope the end result will be rather than seeing the beauty along the way. Progress, on the other hand, says that abundant life isn't found in the end result but in the journey itself.

- In what areas of your life have you felt driven to achieve perfection? How has that turned out for you?

- What are some ways you could aim for progress instead?

- What "messy middle" are you in the midst of right now?

- In what ways are you idealizing the end result of the dream home, family, career, marriage, or friendship, rather than seeing the beauty that's trying to speak to you along the way?

Favorite Nourishing Smoothies

Smoothies are my girls' favorite breakfast and afternoon treat. My oldest daughter said recently, "If I don't have one of your homemade smoothies every day, I feel like I'm going crazy!"

A cold smoothie is also the thing that sounds most appetizing to me after working outside in the field for several hours. The first sip feels like straight liquid gold on those hot, humid summer days. If someone is here helping us on the farm or visiting, they're going to be handed a mason jar with a smoothie inside it too. I've never once had someone turn it down—or refrain from making a slurping noise when their fat straw hits the bottom of the glass.

Smoothies aren't rocket science; making a delicious smoothie is all about proportions. I've finally found the perfect proportions to make a cold, thick but also drinkable-through-a-straw nourishing smoothie. I use a ten-year-old Vitamix blender that's still going strong. Mine was a gift from my mother-in-law when I became a mother. I highly recommend the investment in a good-quality blender, or it will be nearly impossible to get that thick, smooth consistency without burning out the motor. Not that I've ever done that or anything.

GO-TO GREEN SMOOTHIE
Makes 2 servings

2 cups almond or coconut milk

2 frozen whole bananas (if you have a weaker blender, slice them first)

Large handful of kale, spinach, or Swiss chard

2 tablespoons almond or peanut butter

2 tablespoons real-food protein powder

4 to 5 drops natural sweetener, optional

4 to 5 ice cubes

Place all the ingredients in a blender. Before you turn on the blender, make sure the frozen fruit and ice are sticking out above the liquid.

Turn on the blender and slowly increase the speed from low to high, then blend for about 30 seconds or until all the ice and frozen bananas are thoroughly mixed. The smoothie should look like the consistency of soft-serve ice cream.

Pour the smoothie into a large glass with a straw and add any additional toppings desired.

Variation: Minty Green Smoothie

Add 2 to 4 drops of peppermint essential oil to the Go-To Green Smoothie ingredients. I recommend using therapeutic-grade essential oils that are approved for taking internally. I love doTERRA and have used this brand for more than ten years. Alternately, you can use 2 to 4 drops of peppermint extract or a handful of fresh mint from your garden. The mint version of this green smoothie is the only thing my body craves while farming on a really humid Tennessee summer day, and on those days, it's the most refreshing, nourishing thing I can imagine.

CHOCOLATE–PEANUT BUTTER SMOOTHIE

This closely resembles a Wendy's Frosty. I'm just sayin'.

Makes 2 servings

2 cups almond or coconut milk
2 frozen whole bananas (if you have a weaker blender, slice them first)
1 to 2 tablespoons raw cacao
2 tablespoons almond or peanut butter
2 tablespoons real-food protein powder
4 to 5 drops natural sweetener, optional
4 to 5 ice cubes

Place all of the ingredients in a blender. Before you turn on the blender, make sure the frozen fruit and ice are sticking out above the liquid.

Turn on the blender and slowly increase the speed from low to high, then blend for about 30 seconds or until all the ice and frozen bananas are thoroughly mixed. The smoothie should look like the consistency of soft-serve ice cream.

Pour the smoothie into a large glass with a straw and add any additional toppings desired.

CHERRY SMOOTHIE
Makes 2 servings

2 cups almond or coconut milk

1 cup frozen cherries

2 tablespoons almond or peanut butter

2 tablespoons real-food protein powder

4 to 5 drops natural sweetener, optional

4 to 5 ice cubes

Place all of the ingredients in a blender. Before you turn on the blender, make sure the frozen fruit and ice are sticking out above the liquid.

Turn on the blender and slowly increase the speed from low to high, then blend for about 30 seconds or until all the ice and frozen fruit are thoroughly mixed. The smoothie should look like the consistency of soft-serve ice cream.

Pour the smoothie into a large glass with a straw and add any additional toppings desired.

NOTES
- You can use any milk you prefer.
- I use a collagen protein powder made with grass-fed beef collagen, vanilla powder, and monk fruit sweetener. If you don't want to include protein powder, you can add a few tablespoons of hemp seeds.
- Use a sweetener if you prefer a touch of natural sweetness or if you choose to omit the protein powder. I prefer SweetLeaf brand stevia natural sweetener. You can also use a big spoonful of honey or maple syrup.
- Sometimes I put dark chocolate chips at the bottom of my girls' smoothie glasses. The only rule is they have to drink the entire smoothie to the bottom before they get to eat the chocolate chips with a spoon. Win-win!

SMOOTHIE TOPPING OPTIONS
- Ground flaxseed
- Enjoy Life mini chocolate chips
- Cacao nibs
- Ground coconut
- Hemp seeds
- Chia seeds

"

A wise woman takes care of her soul.

And we do have agency. We have

the ability to cultivate joy,

to cultivate delight, to light a candle

in our darkness so we can stay alive.

We have the ability to roll up our sleeves and

write a great story.

—SALLY CLARKSON,
AT HOME WITH SALLY

CHAPTER 9

Learning to Ask for Help

When I was living in Dallas and pregnant for the first time, I prepared for a natural birth at a birthing center. I visualized the entire affair: the midwife, the birthing tub, herbal tea, the giant ball to bounce on, the whole works.

There was no way I could've known that months later, I'd find myself in active labor clinging to a shelf in the body care aisle at Whole Foods, remembering what all the experts had told me: "Create your birth plan, but be prepared to hold it loosely." *Eye roll.*

It ended up being true. I had created what I thought was the bravest and noblest birthing plan for a crunchy, essential-oil-using mama who owned a produce co-op, yet after thirty-six hours of labor at a birthing center, I still hadn't progressed past five centimeters. The pain stripped and cleansed me, forcing out any unsurfaced fears.

I finally admitted, "I need help *now*," and realized that those were the actual bravest words I could say.

In the process of being transferred to the hospital, Steven by my side, I had an earth-shattering contraction in the elevator, scaring a wide-eyed little boy and his parents. After more labor, unbearable pain, an epidural that sent me floating on clouds of chocolate, and the eventual verdict of a C-section, our first daughter, Luci, was removed from my body eight minutes after I entered the operating room.

The first sights and sounds were her robust cry under the fluorescent lights, her arms waving wildly, Korean eyes from her daddy, and a big, wide Italian mouth that looked exactly like my daddy's. At that moment, the way she was brought into the world mattered 0 percent. It just mattered that she was here.

When I brought our baby girl home, my friend Bre lived two blocks down and around the corner, and it was like an actual lifeline was strung between my house and hers, threaded around trees and corners, holding us together. We had been pregnant with our first babies at the same time, and when we were both in our late weeks of pregnancy, Bre taught me how to sew my first pillow out of Anna Maria Horner fabric with pom-pom edging as we leaned precariously over her sewing table, trying to leave space for our swollen bellies.

She gave birth to her son, Jack, two weeks after I had Luci. There we were with our fresh babies, no sleep, and husbands who were away for long hours keeping our family businesses afloat. If either of us needed company and support on a given day, we would text, "I need help. Can you come over?"

The other would arrive with a baby strapped to her chest. We'd take a walk around the block to get our little ones (and our own sleep-deprived minds) some fresh air. We'd sit in one of our living rooms, surrounded by rainbow stacking toys and Melissa & Doug puzzles as we stuffed cloth diapers on autopilot. We shared craft ideas and sewing supplies, and when our babies finally gave in and napped on our chests, we discussed books, recipes, and ideas for how I could be a "real" writer or how she could start an Etsy shop. When Steven came home, my cup was filled on those days versus other days when I'd stayed isolated and counted down the minutes for him to arrive.

Then, our dear friends Tommy and Linda moved two blocks down, and we thought we'd hit the jackpot to have more close friends nearby. We sent sanity-saving texts back and forth: "Meet you on the corner in five minutes for a walk?" Or "What are you guys doing for dinner tonight? We have a pound of chicken sausage, some brown rice, and a bottle of wine . . ."

I walked to Linda's house once, pushing my daughter in my jogging stroller with an unopened bottle of wine in the mesh stroller pocket. She came over one day when I was about to lose my mind and held my baby while I dyed my hair and took a hot bath, two things that helped me feel like a brand-new person a few hours later. And the day Linda's first baby, Bailey, was born at home, I was there in a heartbeat, bringing hot trays of food straight into her kitchen as she recovered on the couch and figured out how to breastfeed.

When I became pregnant with our second daughter, Steven and I couldn't have been more excited. Luci was almost three, and we had been hoping and praying for a sibling for her. Exactly one week after we found out the wonderful news, the rug was pulled from underneath us as a horrific case of all-day pregnancy sickness kicked in, leaving me reeling and utterly helpless.

I'd had bad morning sickness with my first pregnancy, but this was next level. Literally overnight, I could barely take care of myself, much less a husband and an energetic toddler.

I'd never felt nausea this debilitating. That wavy feeling of "I'm going to either puke or die right now" never went away, but my three-year-old daughter still wanted her mommy to play with her and take her to the park as always.

I couldn't go outside for five minutes or even open the refrigerator without dry heaving. There was no rhyme or reason to what would send me running to the bathroom. The best I could do was put on another episode of *Daniel Tiger's Neighborhood* and head back to bed or park myself on the living room chair under a blanket in a fetal position and pray that the minutes would pass quickly.

This behavior was against everything I wanted to be as a woman, mother, and wife. I didn't want the minutes to go too quickly; I wanted to savor them. I didn't want my child to have to stay in the house all day; I wanted her to be free to play and run.

While handling his job at Urban Acres, Steven had also taken on a restaurant consulting gig. On top of that, he was suddenly responsible for grocery shopping, cleaning, and laundry, none of which were his forte.

In my pride, I didn't immediately ask for help. I was much more comfortable being the helper, but that was no longer an option. There were friends who had graciously offered to take our daughter for the afternoon, but I hadn't taken them up on it. There were others who were more than willing to help but just needed to be *asked*.

Finally, Steven firmly yet lovingly suggested, "It's time to ask for help. We can't do this on our own."

That's when Tommy came over and swept the floors. He then proceeded to clean our entire kitchen, declaring that we were no longer using real plates and glasses. The countertop became filled with disposables that would temporarily help us keep our heads above water while one third of our family was completely out of commission. (I hope our current lives as sustainable farmers make up for those few months we contributed to the giant floating island of plastic in the Pacific Ocean and didn't recycle a single thing.)

The first hurdle was *asking*. The second hurdle was receiving and letting go—letting someone else clean my mess, letting my daughter be taken care of by another mother who was feeling perfectly fine.

I need help.

Why are these three small words so difficult to say?

We really don't want to suffer. We don't want to admit that we can't even meet our own basic needs beyond eating Cheerios in red Solo cups or getting dressed for the day in old, dirty lounge pants.

But the truth is, no matter how much we don't want to ask for help, we *cannot* do life on our own. The most character-building moments in our lifetimes are those when we let friends see us at our most vulnerable, allow them to pick us up off the floor, and accept their help without expecting anything in return. Those moments are gold. Vulnerability is essential for connection, and connection to people who truly, deeply know us is lifeblood.

Beautiful things can still unfold in the mess. At the beginning of my sickness, my daughter didn't understand and got frustrated when I was in the bathroom bent over the toilet again. She would bang on the door, or if I left the door open, she would come in and try to pull me away. But Steven and I were determined not to waste this struggle and used it as an opportunity, whenever possible, to teach compassion and empathy. One day, she came into the bathroom and patted my back, saying, "Don't give up, Mommy. It's going to be okay." Another day, she just stood there quietly, balling up pieces of toilet paper and gently dabbing away my tears. (We'll just go ahead and disregard the time she said casually, "Go ahead and frow up, Mommy. I'm gonna eat my breakfast.")

Things eventually got a little better, and after nine weeks of being homebound, I was able to leave the house to take Luci swimming again. I'll never forget that day—the simple joy of the sun on my face and the droplets of water from my daughter's splashes made me tear up for the beauty and gift of being alive and well.

And finally, in the middle of the night in late January, I delivered my second baby girl, Norah, at home in my own bed where I'd suffered and worried for countless hours and months. The sweetness of relief when I held that dark-haired baby in my arms was only magnified by memories of all the people who had helped me and my family survive along the way.

⌒〜⌒

As a farmer, constantly exposed to the elements out here and overwhelmed with more than I can possibly handle, I've learned another level of neediness. Perhaps even more so in the smaller moments than in the monumentally bigger ones, I've been reminded over and over, *It's the people you've been given to walk through life with who matter.*

We've had neighbors trap the raccoon that killed our precious kittens, help us corral escaped farm animals, assist us with planting lettuce, and babysit our children. In turn, we've had the opportunity to invite neighbors over for an impromptu meal, deliver food to farming families when they have a new baby, help replace tractor tires, tear down an old barn, and return a neighbor's escapee horses who were happily munching the grass in our front yard.

A fellow homeschool mom, Julie, and her kids offered to help me plant lettuce when

I was scrambling around frantically before a big farm dinner. She didn't have a clue how to plant lettuce seedlings, but she got her knees dirty with me.

Another homeschool mom, Kendra, saved me hours of time before one of our summer dinners by carefully harvesting and arranging all the table flowers.

My friend Angela showed up several times during our early farm-dinner days to help me stay organized at the entrance so I didn't panic when all the people arrived.

My friend Amy, while visiting from Kentucky, didn't hesitate to jump in and help, weeding one hundred feet of onions with her three-year-old son in tow.

My friend Amber from Austin, while having to corral her toddler to keep him from pulling off the green tomatoes and popping them in his mouth, helped prune and revive our two hundred feet of tomatoes in the scorching August heat.

My friend Melissa, her husband, and four young kids showed up in overalls to help harvest four hundred feet of corn and lay it all out on tables to be dried in neat little rows.

My friend Allison, who lives just seven minutes away, has been a constant source of encouragement, sending me cards in the mail just because, and she doesn't blink an eye when I ask for help with anything—*anything*. I won't forget when she joined my mom from New Jersey and me in pulling insanely heavy silage tarps over the field one fall afternoon before the rains came.

My friend Christy (the one who helped me move) came from suburbia to visit the farm one weekend and ended up broadforking a new lettuce row in her capri jeans.

My brother Glen, my sister-in-law Trish, and my nieces and nephew from Texas were eager to help harvest a bazillion cucumbers and tomatoes in July in the greenhouse, which felt like the surface of the sun. Still, Glen brought his signature playfulness by juggling cucumbers while wearing my daughter's unicorn headband.

I could fill up pages and pages with these people and stories who didn't wait for the perfect clothing, timing, or situation to jump in and get their hands dirty.

And the girl who dabbed my tears on the bathroom floor? She's eleven years old now, with an honest-to-goodness healing presence about her. I've lost count of how many times I've come in from the produce field, covered in dirt and sweat, looking like I'm about to keel over, and she's said, "It's going to be okay, Mommy" as she hands me a glass of water. The younger daughter who was in my belly while I was on the bathroom floor has followed in her sister's footsteps and loves to offer comfort through her healing touch, especially moved when a person is suffering. I hope I can help both my girls learn now when they're young that it's okay—and even wonderful—to be vulnerable, or as Barbara Brown Taylor wrote, "exquisitely vulnerable."[1]

What are you carrying right now that feels heavy and hard? Whatever it is, please know you're not alone. I know what it's like to carry the weight for too long. Maybe it's time to show up for yourself in this moment and realize that "I need help now" are the actual bravest words you can say.

Show up for yourself now because there will come a day when you'll have the opportunity to show up for other people.

One of my favorite authors of all time, Anne Lamott, says that the two best prayers are "Help me, help me, help me" and "Thank you, thank you, thank you."[2]

Preach it, Anne. So many days, I feel like I'm constantly going back and forth between these two prayers, like they're the only things I know how to utter, as though I'm a child just learning to pray.

This is kindred. This is us in our most basic humanity, asking for help when we need it, extending a hand when help is needed, and knowing that we aren't meant to live as islands but as tightly knit communities who care for one another.

While I was writing this book, my seventy-six-year-old dad was rushed to the hospital with COVID-19-induced double pneumonia. My mom, a nurse for more than fifty years, was physically pushed aside from her husband of almost fifty years. She stood there helplessly outside the hospital doors. The medical staff told her to go wait in her car while my dad was wheeled away as he muttered, "Well, I guess this is goodbye . . ."

As she talked to me on the phone from her car in the ER parking lot, tearfully trying to make sense of the trauma they were experiencing, I texted every person I knew: "WE NEED HELP."

Within minutes, a prayer chain for Francis Piccione of Madison, New Jersey, stretched across the United States and even to England. The prayers and support and kindness of believers across the miles and over the phone lines were lifelines.

Miraculously, with the help of swift action and excellent medical care over five days in the hospital, my dad survived and recovered. Due to pandemic restrictions, he was alone in the hospital the whole time, and he burst into tears the moment my mom was able to pick him up at the curb outside the emergency room. We were all changed by it. More vulnerable, yes, but held and bolstered.

A few weeks after that, we found out our oldest daughter had to have inner ear surgery. Having to face the fact that something in her body wasn't working properly was hard enough. Then we had to hand over our daughter to a surgeon for five-plus hours under anesthesia and endure time dragging by endlessly. I had just asked for prayer and support for my dad's emergency illness, and now I had to ask for help again? I felt like the neediest friend ever.

But with every call and text that rolled in, I heard, *You are not alone. She is not alone. God sees you and is with you.* I was grateful that I had sent out the SOS and was able to hold on until the surgery was over. When my baby was wheeled into the recovery room and started fluttering her eyes open again, I was forever changed by it. More vulnerable, yes, but held and bolstered.

This past New Year's Eve, while we were sitting around a table with a few close friends and making toasts of the *good* things that happened in 2020 amid all the hard, my husband, the strongest but also most tender and vulnerable person I know, said it best: "We say we want a life that goes smoothly with no problems in it. But what we really want is to know that we have people who will walk through the hard with us."

Cheers to that.

It's what I learned in the sickness and struggle, in the dirt, in the hospital room, and on the bathroom floor.

We need help.

We need our people.

And a smooth life with no problems in it—but *without* people—isn't one I want to live.

THIS CHAPTER IS ABOUT

Vulnerability

We experience kindred in the stripped-down moments of our humanity, sometimes giving and sometimes receiving.

- What feelings or personal experiences did your mind conjure as you read this chapter?

- "We say we want a life that goes smoothly with no problems in it. But what we really want is to know that we have people who will walk through the hard with us." Write some thoughts on this quote. Do you believe this?

- If you had to choose an easy life alone, or a harder life as part of a tightly knit, authentic community, which would you choose?

"

Courage doesn't always roar. Sometimes courage

is the quiet voice at the end of the day saying,

"I will try again tomorrow."

—MARY ANNE RADMACHER,
COURAGE DOESN'T ALWAYS ROAR

CHAPTER 10

You're Not Gonna Break

My unhealthy view of my body took root sometime in mid-elementary school, when I began to believe that I was overweight for my age. Following that were years of being overly conscious of my appearance and feeling like I was taking up too much space in the world.

Into young adulthood, I abused my body by talking down to it and restricting foods. I criticized it, tried to make it shrink and look better by adorning it with slimming clothes. I took pride in it when it was satisfyingly "small" after I lost fifty pounds in my early twenties. I was insecure about it when it was not "small enough." I was not fully grateful for the body I was given.

Yet that body I criticized and tried to shrink for years did some miraculous things:

It grew and birthed a human. Twice.

Then it grew and birthed a farm. Several times over.

Through both experiences, I gained scars that won't ever go away. My skin may be full of stretch marks and cellulite and sun wrinkles, but my youngest daughter, Norah, says, "Mama, I love your wrinkles. They feel good when I run my fingers over them," and "I love laying my head on your squishy tummy."

I still struggle on days when I let untrue, outside messages into the places they shouldn't be allowed to enter. But I still see that I've come a long way in accepting and loving my body for the way it is, for its inherent value more than its size or appearance.

For the first time in my life, it doesn't hurt so badly when I see the scars and imperfections. I'm honestly proud to be beautifully weathered. I'm proud of the things I've birthed.

After Luci's unexpected C-section birth, I still wanted to try for a natural birth when

I became pregnant for the second time. My midwife was highly experienced in VBAC (vaginal birth after C-section) home births, and she said I was a great candidate. I added more physical activity and chiropractic care and believed this birthing experience would be better and different than the first.

This time, I didn't do it to be noble; I did it because I wanted to try again. *I can do this. I will do this.* I listened to Hypnobabies on loop and wrote the phrase "This is my healing birth" on the mirror in my bedroom in dry-erase marker, whispering it to myself several times a day.

The day finally came in late January when the pangs I'd been having in my lower abdomen were the real thing. My chiropractor, Autumn, who was also my doula, arrived at my house and immediately came to rescue me in my bedroom where I was clinging to the side of my dresser, having a contraction.

For five hours that afternoon and into the evening before my midwife arrived, she supported me through active labor, moving me all over the house in different positions, holding heating pads on my back, rolling essential oils on my ankles, anything and everything I needed her to do. In the background, Steven did everything I needed him to do too; he scurried around the house preparing, lighting candles, managing my birthing playlist, and making me snacks.

I had decided on the front end that I would never say the words "I can't do this anymore" while in labor, because if I did, it would be all over, and I'd be back at the hospital again. Instead, my mantra was, *I can do this. I have to do this. Soon, soon, soon, you'll be holding your baby. You are the only one who can birth this baby.*

By eleven o'clock that night, my water had broken all over my bedroom floor, I'd made it past the point where I'd gotten stalled in labor the first time, and I'd endured the guttural, primal pains of transition. How much harder could it get?

Little did I know that the pushing stage of labor would be *one and a half hours* of the most grueling physical, mental, and emotional work I've ever done in my life to this day, hands down.

I legit thought my body was going to break in two or, at the very least, I was going to push my organs right out. But Doula Autumn was there by my side, holding my left foot in her hand, reassuring me with the most helpful words I've never forgotten: "Don't worry—you're not gonna break. You're not gonna break. You're not gonna break."

Finally, I'd had enough, and in one push, baby Norah shot out so fast that both midwives lunged to catch her. My face was covered with popped blood vessels, my legs felt permanently bent up to my ears, and my chest was sore for days from all the straining. But she was here! The way she shot into the world is the way she's shown up ever since. While we held our girl, the midwives took a photo of the phrase "This is my healing birth" on my bedroom mirror, with us and our new daughter reflected in the background.

Natural birth feels like you're on a train barreling forward at a million miles an hour, and there's no conductor who can stop it but you. You're pushed to the end of your limits, and there's no epidural available to make you feel like you're floating on clouds of chocolate. Unless, of course, there's an emergency, you're not stopping until you're holding a baby in your arms. The train is barreling forward, no matter what.

Norah's birth was the first time I ever did something really hard that I didn't quit—that I wasn't *able* to quit. In that way, it healed me indeed. I vowed I would never again doubt my own strength, physical or otherwise. I would never again take my body for granted.

Just a few years later when I became a farmer, it was time to make good on that promise.

Farming quickly became the hardest physical, mental, and emotional work I'd ever done, second to naturally birthing a baby.

Farming is like going through the labor of childbirth all the time, but there's no baby at the end—just six hundred pounds of cabbage or prolific tomatoes or bushels of cucumbers that are so heavy they break the harvest baskets. This is why farmers take selfies with produce like it's people. We raise the plants from seed and coddle our food babies through wind, frost, sudden heat waves, and the attacks of a myriad of insects. We don't create the life, but we give birth to it again and again. What we're growing and handing over actually feels sacred, even if no one else sees it that way.

That feeling of being on the train barreling forward? That's how the intense physical labor of farm work feels when you're in the middle of it.

Without grit, perseverance, and scrappiness, you just don't survive for very long. There is no avoiding or shortcutting it—unless you quit farming altogether. The soil must be harrowed, the hella-heavy silage tarps must be moved, the fifty- or one-hundred-pound thing must be lifted. Food isn't going to grow itself.

We want the shortcut, the easy way around. We want the benefit of gorgeous lettuce or overflowing bouquets of zinnias without the months and months of careful preparation, struggle, prayer, watching, waiting, prepping, planting, and nurturing. We want the plump, juicy heirloom tomatoes without having to prune them in a 107-degree greenhouse in August while everyone else is at the beach. But it's just not going to happen. Says Robert Frost, "The best way out is always through."[1] We must go *through*—we must dig down deep to learn important lessons like perseverance, grit, and scrappiness.

I just love the Urban Dictionary's definition of a scrappy person: "Someone or something that appears dwarfed by a challenge, but more than compensates for seeming inadequacies through will, perseverance and heart."[2] Being "dwarfed by a challenge" is the story of pretty much my entire life. Time and again, I've shrunken down from challenges or walked away from them altogether, saying, "It's just too hard."

I'm not good at hitting the ball in sixth grade softball? *I'm done with that.*

The kids I'm babysitting never listen to me? *I won't answer that mom's calls again.*

I'm slow at running track? *Bye. I'm hanging up my running shoes.*

I even quit a job as a restaurant hostess one summer during college because people were yelling in my face all night, and the chaotic, fast pace was pretty much a nightmare for an introverted peacemaker like me. After the final straw when a lady chewed me out at the entrance podium during the evening dinner rush, I lied and told my manager I was going back to college sooner than I thought and then got a job folding clothes at Old Navy. True story.

After college, I started to home in on my gifts a bit more, and I did take some big, brave leaps to go after things I truly wanted to do, like moving across the country and taking leadership roles in the music industry. But I still did my best to build a protective cocoon around myself, a life free from conflict and struggle as much as possible.

Then, I married Steven, a headstrong, forward-moving, autonomous visionary. He seems so much stronger than I am. When we're moving our chickens to new pasture in the middle of summer, I'm worried about ticks in the tall grass, standing there with my socks pulled over my jeans and jeans tucked into my tall farm boots, dousing myself with essential oil spray. Steven says, "I eat ticks for breakfast." I freak out because the wood pallet that has to be moved is covered in black widow spiderwebs. He grabs on with bare hands and lifts it with his pinkie. When I let fear have a say, he says, "We've got this. Let's keep going."

But the strength I have to offer is of a different kind—a quiet strength, the calmer, slower-paced, more grounded force. Steven has always been my biggest cheerleader, believing in what I uniquely have to offer as an author, farmer, mom, and woman. What I'm learning now is to face challenges *on my own*, not just because someone is prodding me. I'm learning to be a fighter in the best possible way.

One morning, my new learning was put to a test. I found myself in the position of having to lift an enormous, bulky fifty-pound bag of pelleted chicken fertilizer, which, in case you didn't know, creates one of the most God-awful smells in the universe. The problem wasn't just in lifting it but also in positioning the opening of the bag just right so the fertilizer goes into the bucket and not on your clothes. Steven was off the farm shopping for one of his cooking clients, and my two daughters were off playing in the Forest of Fun.

This was a crucial step in laying a new lettuce row; I had to get it done. So I remembered what I'd learned the day Norah was born.

I dug deep, I channeled "scrappy," grunting louder than was probably necessary, and I lifted that sucker.

I propped the unopened end of the colossal bag on another bucket, which helped brace it while I used every muscle in my arms and abs (thanks, Pilates!) to slowly position the opening to pour the fertilizer into another bucket.

My arms were trembling when it was done, but it worked. And I actually, embarrassingly, yelled, "Heck yeah! Girl power!" really loudly in the middle of our produce field, although no one heard it but me.

That act of grit and perseverance will make all the difference in how the lettuce grows.

This whole seventeen acres of land might seem too much for two people to handle.

It might sound crazy that we sell tickets for 150 people (many times now!) to come eat a multiple-course gourmet dinner on our land without electricity in the middle of a pasture.

It might be insane to get up every Saturday morning at five thirty and sweat down to our underwear by seven thirty, doing farm work while most people are still sleeping.

The blisters, aching muscles, the multitude of bug bites and mounds of muddy laundry—all of it sounds *too hard.*

But there's no *lovely* without the contrast of the *hard.* There just isn't. There's a time to stop and rest and recharge, and there's a time for rolling up our sleeves and getting to work.

I come from a strong woman who doesn't falter easily. My mom can tolerate high levels of pain and spent most of her adult life as a pediatric nurse working twelve-hour night shifts in inner-city hospitals. She does pull-ups—no lie—while holding on to the lifeguard

stand at the community pool with the other half of her body in the water. Even before undergoing a double knee replacement, she hiked and biked and adventured with her grandchildren and helped us shovel an entire driveway full of gravel at age seventy-four.

My children have her DNA as well as the DNA of my strong mother-in-law, who grew up on a farm in South Korea and works like an ox (황소 처럼 일한다 "hwangso cheoleom ilhanda"). She ran her own successful business for thirty-plus years and can outharvest and outwork me any day when she comes and visits the farm.

I intend to keep this going for generations in my two girls, but even after birthing two babies and a farm, I still give in to worry and anxiety. I drive myself crazy. I don't show up for my own life.

Enough.

It's time to remember the power I possess, not just for myself but for the two daughters who are watching me. It's time to remember the strength that comes from my deep faith—my Rescuer treasures me, walks with me, and gives me everything I need.

As I type this, we're about to begin our fifth farming season, the fourteenth spring since we started our first garden in our urban Dallas backyard.

I can see it now. I know what's coming: the dirt in the eyes, the sweaty clothes that are peeled off and thrown directly into the washer, and the muscles that feel like they've run a marathon at the end of the day.

We're usually working eleven-hour days at this time of year to get the planting and event planning done, in addition to our usual jobs of homeschooling, chefing, and writing. Amid it all are the ordinary moments of bike rides at the creek, math lessons, reading *The Lion, the Witch and the Wardrobe* with my girls before bed, "everything in the fridge" soup and cornbread for dinner. I have to take Epsom salt baths every night before bed because my legs ache so much.

One memorable day last spring, after doing all the prep and planting of the zinnias and peppers, I had to lie down on the ground in the middle of the butternut squash row. I felt like I couldn't move another inch.

Lying there, I looked up at the sky and breathed. It was impossibly blue. I imagined plates overflowing with butternut sage ravioli at a future fall farm dinner and people passing dishes down the tables. I saw bouquets of rainbow zinnias like the ones we grew last summer and a surprise bunch of wildflowers in a recycled tin can being delivered on the doorstep of a friend.

I felt simultaneously so small but so loved. I reminded myself of why we're doing this—to create space for connection, for other people to feel loved and known. In all the farming seasons I've lived so far, I've learned that a seed isn't just a seed; it's a catalyst that grows into something much bigger—connection, relationships, beauty. How could I lie down and quit on that?

I got up.

And I kept going.

Because here's the truth: sometimes life is full of things we love, and sometimes it's full of the hard things that must be done to keep the things we love. We get to choose: Will we walk through those hard things, trusting that something good is waiting in the middle of them *and* on the other side?

It may feel like we're gonna break, like we'll be torn in two. The pain is real—it will cleanse and strip us, and we won't be the same. But "though we experience every kind of pressure, we're not crushed. At times we don't know what to do, but quitting is not an option. . . . God has not forsaken us. We may be knocked down, but not out."[3]

None of us wants suffering, but God *never* leaves us. And as long as we're still on this earth, he also gives us flesh-and-blood people to walk alongside us in our struggles. I'm actually not "the only one who can birth this baby." I'm so grateful for the wise and inspiring women in my life who "doula" me, who remind me of truth when I need a nudge—or huge shove—in the right direction. Sometimes we just need someone to come alongside us, hold our feet, cheer us on, and remind us, "I see how hard this is for you. But please, keep breathing and hang in there. You're not gonna break."

I hope you have someone who will do that for you, but just in case, I've written it here so you can open this page anytime you need the reminder:

Though you may feel afraid and shaky at times, this skin you're living in is a gift. You are stronger than you think you are. You have the strength of the God of the universe pulsing through you.

You're not gonna break.

You're not gonna break.

You, my friend, are not gonna break.

THIS CHAPTER IS ABOUT

Strength

We are often stronger than we think we are and more capable than we realize.

- When is a time you felt you were going to break? Who was with you? How did you pull through it?

- Have you ever felt God was giving you supernatural strength, either directly or through the encouragement of another person?

- Name a time when you felt really strong or brave, even if you still felt scared out of your mind. When and where was it, and what were you doing?

- Write down three of the hardest things you've ever done. How were they worth it? How did you grow?

"

We seek the change that is interesting,

the change for the better, and most of all,

the change that connects

us to someone else.

—SETH GODIN,
WHAT TO DO WHEN IT'S YOUR TURN
(AND IT'S ALWAYS YOUR TURN)

CHAPTER 11

That Saturday Morning Feeling

Apparently, I do canning now. Canning and preserving are things I once said I don't do, along with running, diets, competitive sports, and making my bed. Now I guard our arsenal of jams and rainbowy pickled things on the barn shelves like they're actual hard-won treasure.

And they are—the tangible, jewel-toned results of months of labor, jars infused with heritage and stories.

But I didn't always see them that way.

By the end of our first farming season in 2017, we were still on a high from all that had unfolded, culminating with the magic of our first farm dinner that October. But it was already time to start thinking about next season.

A few things were abundantly clear:

1. We were more tired, yet more fulfilled, than we could've ever imagined.
2. We loved interacting with our customers and "regulars," but driving all over God's creation making the rounds at farmers markets was definitely not how we wanted to spend our precious time—or our family's time.
3. We knew we could create beautiful food, gather people, and grow nourishing things.
4. This land—and the fruits of it—were meant to be shared.

There were plenty of other gifted local and sustainable farmers, including several just down the road from us, who had CSAs and farmers market setups all over town. We didn't need to try to be them; we needed to put our own spin on things, to give the unique gifts *we* had to offer.

What if we started a farm store on our own property? What if we welcomed people in here not just a few times a year at our farm dinners but every weekend?

We knew retail. We'd done it for years and had built a loyal customer base of thousands, but we'd also learned some hard lessons about inconsistency we didn't want to have to relearn. If we were going to commit to doing retail again, it would have to be different from before.

So we decided that we'd open our own farm store, and during our main farming season of April to October, we would be open every single Saturday from 9:00 a.m. until noon, whether one person came or a hundred.

Over the course of the winter leading into 2018, we worked on transforming the smaller Amish-built cedar shed that was just a few steps outside our back door in front of the produce field. I became well acquainted with the nail gun while Steven sawed pieces of barn wood to create a wooden accent wall. Our girls helped paint the other walls and gallivanted back and forth to the barn for supplies in between runs to Fairy Creek to play, climb, or ride the tree swing.

After the walls went up, we hung repurposed wooden pallets for shelves to display our logo T-shirts and trucker hats. I wielded the chalkboard paint mercilessly on the insides of all the doors, unwilling to wait another minute to put my own unique flourish on them—handwritten inspirational quotes, little drawings, and lists of all the bountiful things we'd be offering up for sale.

As far as products, we knew we didn't need to do *everything*; we just needed to do a few things really, really excellently. So we did what any sane foodie farmpreneur would do and started with our greatest hits, the two original recipes that had never failed to make people happy at our Urban Acres farmstead in Dallas: homemade cinnamon rolls and homemade granola. We decided we would give cinnamon rolls away for *free* to anyone who came to the farm store on Saturday mornings.

At the end of April 2018, we officially opened. We had no idea if anyone would come.

Some Saturdays we had a small crowd, and some? *Crickets.* But there was still the same amount of work no matter what. On those days, I wondered if this whole thing was a bad idea. Why had we committed to doing this every single Saturday, again?

Steven, ever the maverick, was unfazed. He reminded me that we needed to stick to the plan and move forward as a family, as a team. When it was still dark on Saturday mornings, he baked up a storm, making pillowy, ooey-gooey cinnamon rolls slathered with thick, warm icing that made the commercial kitchen smell heavenly for hours. We made batches and batches of our "Perfect Granola"—a balanced mix of crunchy, salty, and sweet—and spread out samples in little plastic cups.

Our girls knew that every Friday morning and afternoon, we'd be prepping for the farm store: harvesting, washing, packaging. After washing the lettuce in giant tubs, I put it—literally—on the spin cycle in our new washing machine turned salad spinner and packaged it into clamshells so our customers would have the freshest salads on their tables the next day. The girls stuck alongside me, gathering the most vibrant zinnias or sunflowers in buckets, handing me rubber bands or taking turns carefully plucking off cherry tomatoes like giant golden beads. There were bundles of magenta radishes in the spring, turquoise paper baskets of cucumbers and tomatoes in the summer, overflowing piles of butternut squash in the fall.

Throughout the week, in the midst of homeschooling and Steven's private chef work, we were also launching a wholesale business for our Buttery Sweet Salad Mix. The salad mix had been the item customers had requested most when we'd been at the farmers markets, selling out every single week. So in addition to growing it for our farm store and dinners, we decided to create a new facet of our business to grow for local stores and restaurants.

After earning our organic certification—a huge feat!—our salad mix was on the fast-track to being in our local and regional Whole Foods. We'd spent thousands of dollars on the infrastructure and supplies to amp up lettuce production and had even brought on a business partner and interns.

Meanwhile, the farm store was gaining momentum. Word started spreading, and more and more people were coming on Saturdays. They'd heard about the cinnamon rolls. They'd tasted the granola and were coming to get multiple bags of it because they couldn't be without it in their pantry. They said they'd never tasted lettuce as good as our Buttery Sweet Salad Mix and craved it every day now.

This thing was working, and though it was a big challenge, I truly enjoyed it. Soon, the sound of gravel rumbling as a car pulled in the entrance became one of my new favorite sounds. I was like a giddy child on Christmas, using all my self-control to welcome people and not pounce on them: *I wonder who it is? Will it be a return customer or someone new?* Each car door opening was another surprise, another unique person with their own unique stories.

Throughout the season, we kept hosting Kindred Dinners, which were selling out every single time. Steven was able to incorporate many of our farm products into what he was creating in the kitchen, and his private chef clients kept growing rapidly. After years of practicing his craft, his distinctive Southern/Korean style was shining through like never before.

But as 2018 rambled on, the wholesale program wasn't working well. The delicate lettuce had to be coddled with sprinklers and row covers in Tennessee's intense heat and humidity. We couldn't seem to get the right balance of supply and demand. The process of getting our lettuce approved for retail in a national chain was stressful, to say the least, and we didn't have the resources to get there. Farming for our own supply was one thing; growing wholesale was another beast altogether.

It was time for a come-to-Jesus meeting: we knew the wholesale thing felt all wrong. We weren't farming so we could pump out a bunch of lettuce to go on a grocery store shelf and then into a nameless person's basket. Growing beautiful lettuce for stores and restaurants was a great goal; it just wasn't our goal. Although it was traumatic and painful for all of us, we dissolved the business partnership.

We followed the arrows; we had seen the connections that were being made with people in the community on Saturdays and at our dinners. The facets of our business that were succeeding were built around the things we loved and were doing from the heart.

It was time to clearly define our lane: bringing together the culinary with farming to create opportunities for people to experience peace, connection, and community. We want everyone who comes here to be able to slow down, exhale, and take a piece of "kindred" with them, wherever they go.

Since then, we haven't looked back, and everything we grow stays on the farm until someone takes it home in their own two hands or eats it on a plate.

By saying yes to opening the farm store, we said yes to consistency, responsibility, and hospitality.

We have to get up early every Saturday morning, when sometimes we'd rather be drinking coffee in bed.

We have to constantly reinvent ways to keep our girls engaged, giving them each special roles and "jobs" so they can have a part in the process and feel pride in accomplishing something. They learn things by watching and doing that they can't learn on paper—like the value of hard work, the value of a dollar, the skill of entrepreneurship—all while still under our protective wings.

We're used to hosting friends in our home at this point—we've done it since Luci was nestled in one arm while I ate with my free hand at our dining room table stuffed with friends. But welcoming strangers is a different kind of hospitality. Our girls have to learn how to converse with people of all ages, look people in the eye respectfully, speak confidently. With appropriate supervision, of course, they give farm tours and accurately explain our farm processes: how we plant in the field, how we take care of the animals, and how the greenhouses work. As a result, we continue to see their natural talents unfurl. Norah, more extroverted, gives awesome farm tours. Luci, more reserved and detailed, loves helping behind the scenes. Both love creating beautiful table displays.

The same motto that's served Steven and me since the beginning of our marriage still applies: work together as a team, and celebrate and respect our separateness within the team.

We work hard, and then on Saturday evenings and Sunday, we Sabbath hard. We rest, recharge, play, and enjoy the fruits of our labor. We fuel up for the week ahead, and then we do it all over again.

The work of building a sustainable farm isn't a quick turnaround; it's a labor of love. By investing into the soil and slow processes that create our artisan goods—jams, pickles, sauces, kimchi, healing hand salves—we are investing in people. We're stewarding stories.

Ya know, as the saying goes: "The couple who jars jam at midnight together stays together." I won't forget the night we made heirloom tomato jam, and Steven tasted it and said it needed some umami. At the last minute, he added some gochujang (Korean red pepper paste), and it was just the thing to take it over the edge from average to bombshell.

So yes, even though it's still kinda stressful and overwhelming to me, *you better believe* I do canning now. Hundreds and hundreds of jars, each carrying memories of where the ingredients came from and of late nights with Steven, both of us silly and delirious, filling the containers with hot, syrupy liquid.

Strawberry Serrano and Strawberry Balsamic Thyme: made with ripe, fragrant strawberries from Farmer Ben, who mentored us in farming when we first arrived in Tennessee.

Blueberry Basil and Blueberry Lavender: made with blueberries from a farm down the road, our own basil, and lavender grown by a beloved farm store regular who brought it over one day as a surprise.

Peach Chipotle and Peach Bourbon Vanilla: made with local peaches and a special gifted bourbon.

Apple Pie: made from apples we picked ourselves, while simultaneously sweaty like summer and breezy like fall, with our daughters one October day on a farm an hour away in Alabama.

Sicilian Tomato, Tomato Bacon, and Heirloom Tomato Gochujang: made with one flavor each for the three cultures that have formed us—Sicilian, Southern, Korean.

The kimchi tells stories of Steven's mom, who grew up on a potato and rice farm in South Korea and loves passing her traditions on to us. She drove all the way from Dallas to help us transform our Napa cabbage into kimchi made with her as-authentic-as-it-gets family recipe. It's great to grow cabbage, and it's great to make kimchi, but we're just plucky enough to do both, and

it makes it even more special that kimchi-making has been happening in our family for generations. People come from all over, asking for the probiotic-rich, gut-friendly goodness, saying they're mixing it in with their eggs, putting it on burgers, or eating it every day straight from the jar.

Our salves tell stories of calendula seeds started in February, seedlings planted in April, and first flowers harvested in early June, making fingertips smell heavenly. It's dried over the summer and steeped into olive oil for six weeks on a sunny windowsill, warmed with beeswax into salve in the fall that will help heal someone's skin all winter. When everything is dead and brown again, we'll rub some into our dry, cracked hands and into the hands of our children at bedtime. We'll make healing tea from the dried flowers, and it'll warm us down to our toes.

The miracle is not lost on us.

In early spring 2020, the coronavirus hit middle Tennessee for the first time, right before we were about to open for the season.

Like all other farmers and business owners, we were forced to adjust and pivot to survive. We added online ordering so local customers could still come and safely pick up their farm-fresh goodies and comfort foods from coolers and tables set up under tents in our driveway while we waved to them across the field. We still greeted them by name and shouted, "We miss seeing you!"

As people were cautiously released from quarantine by early summer, we were able to open up the farm store again. Even with the adjustments of the COVID-19 world, people still came—more than ever. We kept everything outside under a tent for safety purposes, which ended up being an unexpected blessing. Instead of being cramped inside the tiny farm store building, there was plenty of space.

Kids ran free. Grown-ups ran free. We met so many new friends and neighbors in addition to our beloved regulars.

The world we knew had changed. But there was more clarity than ever: humans will always need fresh air, freedom, beauty, adventure, face-to-face connection, flowers, playfulness, and, yes, even treats sometimes.

Physical isolation, smartphones, computer screens, and social media can never fill holes that were meant to be filled with real human experiences.

We ended the summer with something we'd never done before—a Saturday morning pop-up breakfast. It was Steven's idea; I, of course, thought it was too risky. With all our preplanned, heavily staffed, ticketed farm dinners we'd successfully pulled off, we'd never done this type of event before and had no idea what the response would be. We posted a menu on social media and said we'd have cinnamon rolls, homemade biscuits with jam, and three different kinds of breakfast tacos. All of it would come out hot, to order.

At nine o'clock the next morning, the parking lot was filled with cars, and a socially distanced line of people, longer than we'd ever had before on a normal day, zigzagged around our little farm store table.

My heart was beating fast as I took orders and rang people up. Our six-year-old ran orders to the kitchen all the way across the produce field. Steven whipped up every single order by himself, and our ten-year-old ran them from the kitchen back to the farm store.

It was nuts. We had no staff for this one, just a family of four working their tails off and doing their best to pump out delicious tacos, biscuits, and cinnamon rolls and create space for people to feel nourished and welcomed.

Customers spread out under shade trees with picnic blankets and lawn chairs and walked leisurely around the farm. Kids played in the Forest of Fun. The weariness from months of quarantining, shocking news, and health worries dripped visibly off their bodies, lightening the load a little.

After the last person left at noon, you should have seen our commercial kitchen! *Um, whoa.* We were cleaning up for days, but we were all on an adrenaline high: "Can you *believe* what we just did?" Our girls were proud of themselves. I was proud of us.

The final count that day:

- 100 homemade cinnamon rolls
- 100 homemade breakfast tacos
- 50 homemade biscuits
- Way more people than we expected, who were looking for a little farm adventure on a Saturday morning
- A family of four extremely grateful for the gift of this place

You'd think I'd have learned by now.

I shy away from risk. I squash ideas that might require me walking through the fire. Yet every time I push through the hard things with my people toward a good and worthy goal, it always creates abundance and fullness of life in some way.

"Together" is the best place to do hard things. Every single time.

Remember "That Saturday Morning Feeling" Steven and I experienced on the Texas back roads? Up early, hot drink in hand, driving to a local farm to pick up some fresh produce and baked goods and to take a break from the busyness of the city for a bit . . .

Now we're owners of a farm that people drive to on Saturday mornings, and we do not take that lightly. We meet people like:

Jack and Jeanette, the couple from New Jersey who lives down the road and reminds me of my Italian relatives—same accent, same food memories, same jokes.

Ruth, who always brings us dried lavender from her garden in mason jars carefully labeled *Culinary* or *Fragrance Only* and makes lavender sachets to be tucked under our pillows.

Chaz, who brings his young daughter on a Saturday morning date to our farm to pick up granola and cinnamon rolls.

The little boy who got out of the minivan before the rest of his family and immediately ran full tilt to the row of zinnias. After coming to a screeching halt, he momentarily lost himself in a swarm of butterflies.

Kim, who strolled up on U-Pick Flower Day with butcher paper already formed into a cone to hold the flowers she was going to deliver to a friend afterward. She walked through hundreds of flowers, selecting just the right ones.

The man who told us that our biscuits were the best he'd ever had and not to tell his grandma.

Garrett and Hannah, who, after not coming around for a while, suddenly showed up with a newborn baby in a carrier on Hannah's chest. They walked straight over to the zinnias to show them to their new, wide-eyed baby girl.

And Katherine, who always stocks up on salad greens and hasn't missed a single Kindred Dinner. We can always find her at the table by following the sound of hearty laughter.

And so many more. Being part of their lives in some way—even for a few hours on a Saturday—is seriously such a joy. And it's perhaps more meaningful because we've been on the other side of this. We know what it's like to jump in the car after a long week, seeking peace and space and freedom, and to show up someplace new, with souls and stomachs ready to be filled.

We can give them what we craved back then on the Texas back roads.

They come to learn; we give them a tour through greenhouses filled with seeds and trellises bursting with tomatoes.

They come to have fun; we give them tree swings, flower picking, and space to lay their picnic blankets in the sun.

They come to slow down and escape stress; we invite them to wander in wide-open spaces, letting the meadows and bees and butterflies speak.

They show up with a desire to be fed; we give them the best, tastiest things we can make and grow and something to take home—a bag of granola, a jar of jam, a memory.

We don't give them perfect, fancy, or curated.

We give them real. We give them kindred.

THIS CHAPTER IS ABOUT
Community

Something beautiful can be built that the community can enjoy, but it will take consistency and responsibility, even when it's hard.

- Have you ever been a part of a community experience like I describe in this chapter?

- Which part of the story resonated most with you?

- Do you believe that "together" is the best place to do hard things? How have you experienced it?

- What is a way you can take on something hard with your own people to work toward a good and worthy goal? What abundance are you hoping it will create?

- Instead of aiming for perfect, fancy, or curated, how can you give people "real"? How can you give them "kindred"?

Strawberry Rosé Jam

Yeah, I know . . . I thought canning and preserving was intimidating, too, remember? So to take away some obstacles here, we're going to make this as a refrigerator jam so you don't actually have to can anything.

Block out a few hours to try this recipe yourself, sipping the remainder of the wine from the bottle, of course. Or grab a few friends and figure this out together. When you're done, you will look at the gemlike jars with awe and wonder, seeing them for the treasures that they are.

Makes approximately 6 half-pint jars

2 cups spring-ripe strawberries, sliced in half, tops removed
2 cups sugar
1/4 cup fresh lemon juice
2 cups rosé wine
1/4 teaspoon cracked black pepper
1 package fruit pectin, optional

In a large saucepan, combine the strawberries, sugar, lemon juice, rosé, and pepper. Cook over medium-high heat and bring to a boil.

Reduce the heat until the mixture reaches a simmer, and cook until the mixture thickens to a jam-like consistency. While you're cooking, a great way to test the thickness of your jam is to put a plate in the freezer for a few minutes, then remove the plate and put a spoonful of jam on it. Run your finger through the jam. Does your finger make a clear line straight through the jam? If so, your jam is thick enough. If it doesn't make a clear line and looks runny, you can add some pectin.

If using pectin, bring your jam back to a boil and add the pectin. Stir well to incorporate the pectin and cook for 1 minute. Then remove from the heat and let it cool a bit.

You made jam! Put your jam in mason jars, let it cool, and store in the fridge for up to 3 months.

SERVING SUGGESTIONS

- Spread the jam on biscuits or sourdough bread.
- Add a scoop of jam on top of ice cream.
- Spread some of the jam on homemade pizza, mixing it with the tomato sauce.
- Add the jam to a sandwich with mayo.
- Spread the jam over goat cheese or brie on a charcuterie board.

"

We are all more capable

than we realize of creating

a life of whimsy

and adventure.

—MARIA GOFF,
LOVE LIVES HERE

CHAPTER 12

Ice Cream on the Roof

When I first met Steven, he and his younger sister, Michelle, already had this little motto between them: *It's all about the memories.*

It's what prompted them to drop everything one summer and drive twenty-two hours and forty-five minutes from their Dallas suburb all the way to New York City, buy last-minute tickets in Times Square, and end up sitting in *the front row* of *Les Misérables* on Broadway, face-to-face with Éponine.

But I wasn't totally sold on "it's all about the memories" quite yet. I was, oh, about 85 percent into it. The other 15 percent of me couldn't help but be concerned with the details and logistics of every possible scenario.

Yeah, I love living for memories, but I'm not all *about it. Can't we just make a few plans? Know what to expect? Have a few days' notice so I can make sure my laundry is clean and packed nicely into a suitcase?*

I was a young woman who'd had her share of adventures by then, sure, but I was still tightly wound and bound to everyday responsibilities. I was still choosing safe instead of brave, predictable instead of possible.

One of the earliest adventures I remember is when one summer evening in grade school, my parents announced a surprise. After they had previously told my brother and me that we were *not* going to be taking a vacation to Williamsburg, Virginia, like we did every summer, they said we were getting up the very next morning, loading up our green Plymouth Volare station wagon and going to Williamsburg after all—for an entire *week*!

And if that wasn't enough, we were going with my best friend since birth, Jason, and his family. I shrieked and ran to my room to pack my bags—there was just enough time to corral my Barbies, books, and road trip games for the unexpected vacation we were leaving on *tomorrow morning*.

We spent the next week exploring "countries" at Busch Gardens, playing mini golf, and eating inordinate amounts of silver-dollar pancakes and steak sticks at the Shoney's breakfast bar. I stayed at the hotel pool into the dusky evening with Jason, doing cannonballs off the diving board and swimming until our eyes were bloodshot. We walked back to our rooms barefoot with pine needles sticking to the bottoms of our feet.

Then, one summer day in middle school, my mom declared that she was sick and tired of going to Williamsburg, Virginia, every year. She handed me an envelope with tickets for the two of us to go on a trip for the first time together—to *Ireland*. My dad didn't want to fly, and my brother was away at college. Neither she nor I had ever been overseas before. Sure, we *could* have had a travel planner arrange the whole itinerary for us so we could stay in safe, predictable chain hotels. Instead, we left most of the trip unscheduled and stayed in bed-and-breakfasts hosted by local Irish families because my mom wanted us to experience "the real Ireland." And the real Ireland, in many ways, seemed right out of a PBS film, full of magic and mystery.

Although I felt nervous not knowing what to expect each day and was forced out of my comfort zone as a moody eleven-year-old, the trip stretched and formed me in good ways. I couldn't possibly forget the unique culture of the places—and people—we encountered as we got lost multiple times, stayed in a haunted mansion in a thunderstorm, and stood on the edges of the Cliffs of Moher listening to flautists and harpists sending their music into the wind.

Right after Steven and I got married, I went back to Nashville for a short business trip.

My old roommate Suz and I decided to do something we'd wanted to do ever since we became friends: wake up at 6:00 a.m. on an ordinary Friday; throw an iPod (hello, 2006), our bathing suits, apples, and peanut butter crackers into a bag; hop into Suz's green Jeep nicknamed "Boy Scout"; and drive to one of our favorite places, the emerald coast of Florida.

After working extra hours the day before for my job at Mocha Club, I was graciously granted that Friday off. Sure, we *kinda sorta* planned it the night before, but our adventure still felt a little brazen, a little risky in our still conservative way—two single girls on the open road in a Jeep pointed toward the coast while everyone else was at work on a weekday.

Five hundred miles, many laughs, and one emergency bathroom stop later, we drove into Seaside wearing perma-grins on our faces and flip-flops that were itching to be removed so our toes could sink into the sugar-white sand. Even though—and perhaps *because*—it was less than forty-eight hours long, that trip will go down as one of my all-time favorite adventures: a weekend full of beach combing, shopping at outdoor markets, and eating ice cream cones with my friend. When I left to fly back home to Texas, I was fishing for my boarding pass at the airport and found sand in my purse.

What do you think of when you think of adventure?

It's easier for me to think of the obvious examples: traveling from village to village on the Italian Riviera, collecting rocks and seashells; driving through the raw, unspoiled beauty of the European countryside with my mom or dangling our legs over the edge of the Grand Canyon; hiking an unexplored trail in New Mexico with Steven without another soul for miles.

But what about the not-so-obvious ones? The ones where we *don't* have to go hundreds or thousands of miles from home?

Shortly after we moved to Tennessee and lived in the rental house, we were desperate for something to do with two little energetic kids on the weekend. We'd heard Middle Tennessee had a ton of waterfalls, and I'd been to a few of them back in college.

And that's how Sunday Fundays were born. Sunday afternoons after church quickly became reserved for chasing as many Tennessee waterfalls as possible within a two-hour radius, practically a new one every weekend. We learned how to expertly pack supplies for a day trip with a toddler and a five-year-old and that waterproof hiking shoes were pricy but absolutely worth every penny.

We didn't wait for the stage of life to be perfect. Instead, we packed bathing suits and hiking clothes into our backpacks, changed in the church bathroom, and walked back out in our Keens and Chacos.

The excitement and playfulness that unfolded in our family during these waterfall trips kept us going while we transitioned to a whole new life, a new state, new friends. And it drew us together.

We discovered that Old Stone Fort has a secret, quicker passageway to the falls, with one caveat: you have to scale an almost-vertical boulder. You should have seen the teamwork it required to pull that off with a toddler in a backpack, but once we were down there, it was like we'd suddenly been transported to a magical cove in Hawaii. There wasn't another soul there, and we were surrounded by waterfalls so powerful that the pounding water left bruises on my shoulders the next day.

When friends from Texas came to visit, we couldn't *wait* to show them all our waterfall discoveries. On a Sunday afternoon in late September, we went to one we hadn't visited before—Rutledge Falls—and because it was no longer summer, none of us had bathing suits with us.

To heck with being dry. When we saw that big, welcoming swimming hole and the falls pounding over rocks low enough to sit on, we went for it. We all jumped in with our clothes on—two four-year-olds, an eight-year-old, three late-thirties adults, and me, who had just turned forty. We were soaked down to our underwear, with no change of clothes. I had runny mascara raccoon eyes for the rest of the afternoon. It was exhilarating.

When we moved to the farm and were getting settled into our historic 1940s digs, we soon realized that the pitch of the roof just outside the schoolroom window seemed to be slanted *just* right—and there was a window that opened right onto it. Steven and the girls simultaneously proclaimed one evening, "Let's go out on the roof!"

The first time we tried it, I was certain my children were going to fall to their demise on the lawn below, even though I held their forearms in a death grip and wouldn't let them venture two inches past the windowsill. Steven, ever the daredevil, was already around the corner, where I could no longer see him, scoping out whether we could go higher up. The roof shingles are so abrasive, there's no way a person could have easily rolled down the gradual pitch, but I still laid a bath towel beneath us for more traction. The four of us finally settled into our precarious positions. We sat and looked around.

Whoa.

In the pitch black, the sky opened like a planetarium. The navy outline of the Tennessee hills surrounded us. We could see the tops of cars and trucks whizzing by on our country road, but they couldn't see us.

I reached one arm back inside the window and grabbed the telescope from the corner of the schoolroom. Five minutes later, we were not only perched on the roof overlooking Santa Fe but also gazing at *actual, real Saturn with rings around it.* I'll never forget that feeling of awe.

Our first summer after moving to the farm, my friend Christina from Dallas was visiting with her husband and two kids. After days of helping us on the farm collecting eggs, planting thousands of lettuce seedlings, and pulling up old basil plants and hurling them off the back of the pickup truck into the pig pasture, we were exhausted.

Our kids and husbands were finally in bed, and we had been holding out to enjoy the pint of Jeni's Splendid Ice Cream that was calling to us from the freezer.

"So . . . ready for ice cream?" I asked.

"Of course!" she answered. "And . . . didn't you mention that you've been on the roof before? Let's take our ice cream up there."

Of all the times we'd been on the roof, I'd never thought to bring ice cream.

A generous bowl of ice cream on a humid summer Tennessee night? *Pretty delightful.*

A generous bowl of ice cream on a humid summer Tennessee night . . . while sitting on a slightly dangerous, slanted roof with a friend, overlooking a country sky full of stars? *Exponentially better.*

So how do we find adventure right where we are?

The answer is this: in the ordinary extraordinary moments *with our people.*

When I think back to all the adventures I've been on in my life—whether on a remote rural road in Ireland or my own slanted roof in Santa Fe—it was a special person or group of people by my side who made it wonderful.

Nope, I don't just want adventure. I want a *shared* adventure.

Realizing adventure isn't about a particular place but the people I'm with, I'm able to release the need for predictability and just *let go.*

Rediscovering and releasing the girl inside who so deeply desires to live more riskily and bravely, I'm able to be swept up in all the adventures in front of me, in my own everyday life, right now.

As much as rhythms and seasons heal us and bring stability to our days, adventures remind us that we're fully alive and that it's okay—and, yes, even *necessary*—to break the rules sometimes. They show us that sharing risky experiences in the everyday unknown strengthens our relationships and binds us to one another in unforgettable ways.

However big or small, near or far, adventures with our people lead to the best stories, the ones we tell over and over. These are the stories that quicken our insides because they actually happened. These are the stories that build a legacy, the ones we'll tell our grandchildren thirty years later, the ones that feel like magic.

Remember the first time we sat on the roof and saw Saturn?

Remember that time Mommy jumped into the waterfall with her clothes on?

Remember when Daddy turned the living room into a movie theater, with a roped-off ticket line, handwritten tickets, and buttery popcorn?

Remember when we pulled the comforters off our beds to pile in the back of the pickup truck at the drive-in movie theater?

Remember when we turned that giant tarp into a Slip 'N Slide for the Fourth of July? And the kimchi tub into a kiddie pool?

Adventures we share—especially the ones that are scary in the best possible ways— are permanently seared into our memories, glowing, conveniently allowing the actual scary parts to fade away with time because we went through something together. We took a risk, faced an unknown, made a discovery. We did something crazy and lived to tell the tale.

Let's do more of this.

There's a time to let our kids play, and there's a time to jump in the water with our clothes on and get wet. There's a time for eating our ice cream at the table, and there's a time for taking it out on the roof (although I much prefer the roof now).

God gave us flowers to pick and mountains to climb and oceans to swim. But we're also being invited on an adventure in the way we embrace life, even in the ordinary places—the backyards, the minivans, the makeshift forts in the living room.

I want to be a person who chooses the adventure because these beautiful, messy places are where life is lived. And a few moments of getting wet or dirty or lost or scratchy or road-weary are worth the connection and the memories. Always.

THIS CHAPTER IS ABOUT
adventure

However big or small, adventures, especially in our ordinary lives with our people, lead to the best stories and memories, the ones we tell over and over. Let's fill our lives with more of those moments.

- Name a time you felt free and wild, uninhibited, fully yourself.

- Is there something you've always wanted to do or try but haven't ever done? Why?

- Write down four specific time slots in a month when you could add in some kind of adventure. If you think there's no empty time slot, what can you eliminate or move around to carve out time?

- Think of things you do on an ordinary basis—the way you eat your meals or spend your weekends or even your weeknights. How can you add an element of adventure to make these things a little more special and unexpected?

Food and adventure pairings

- Get some pints of your favorite ice cream and eat it on the roof on a clear night.

- Take your favorite cookies and a thermos of cold milk to an overlook or other spot where you can view the sunset.

- Pack a picnic lunch and eat it by a creek or river or at the base of a waterfall.

- Have a backyard campout and roast hot dogs and make s'mores.

- Go to a drive-in movie theater and eat popcorn and snacks in the back of your truck or the back of your car with the trunk open.

"

You must not ever stop being **whimsical**. And you must not, ever, give anyone else the **responsibility** for your life.

—MARY OLIVER,
UPSTREAM

CHAPTER 13

The Speed of Listening

The slow unfolding and unraveling of time is a necessary ingredient for the health of all living things:

- seasons
- bread dough rising
- flower petals
- sunrises
- pregnancies
- the cycles of the moon
- fruit trees maturing
- childhood

"Time, slow down!" It's every parent's lament. We've all felt it in some way—the slipping of time through our fingers like sand through a sieve, the ticking by of minutes and days that unravel quickly into years and decades.

Wasn't I just a naive, wide-eyed freshman showing up at college orientation in my jean shorts and maroon lipstick?

Weren't we just newlyweds, decorating our first apartment with hand-me-downs?

Wasn't I just a bleary-eyed new mom toting my newborn around the house in a sling, hoping for a nap longer than thirty minutes?

And when did my baby go from barely speaking words to asking about things like "Where do fairies live?" And "What makes cars go?" And "What's it like to live in Africa?"

One minute, I had a toddler with arm rolls and a penchant for sneaking chocolate chips from the cupboard at breakfast time; the next minute, I had an eleven-year-old nose-deep in *Harry Potter*, wearing pajama pants in the middle of the day and drinking tea.

The thing is, though, we do *have* time. In one single day? 86,400 seconds. In an average lifetime? Over two billion moments.

But where does it go? Is time really passing too quickly? Or are we just not savoring the time we have?

In the New Jersey suburban neighborhood where I grew up, my mom modeled what it was like to literally stop and smell the roses (or the crocuses). While other children and parents walked by, unnoticing, she always stopped and pointed out the hardy crocuses blooming outside the window of my kindergarten classroom. In my 1980s maroon corduroy pants, I squatted down to examine their purple-and-yellow tips poking eagerly through the early spring soil.

I can't thank my mom enough for that legacy. These encouragements toward beauty, time, and slowness—even though she worked full time as a pediatric nurse—stood out to me. Before I even became a mother, I thought of the childhood I wanted to help create for the children I hoped I'd have one day. More than anything, I wanted *time* with them. Time to be present, to see beauty, to explore, to be there when they took their first steps and said their first words.

From the moment I became a mother, I always worked other jobs (and still do!). I became frazzled with all I was trying to juggle—like on the days I looked at myself in the mirror for the first time at 1:43 p.m. and scared myself. (*What the . . . ? How long has my hair looked like this?*) All I wanted those days was to crash into bed, or at the very least take a hot bath by myself with the rubber duckies wearing bowties, terry cloth puppets, and California Baby shampoo.

It felt forever away when I had a baby and a three-year-old, but I knew the time would eventually come when I'd talk about "when the children were little." I knew one day onesies would be gone for good, diapers would be a burden of the past, and we'd wish we had puzzle pieces and crayons and Sophie the Giraffe to pick up off the floor before going to bed. The days of when we had small children would all be one big, beautiful memory, their childhoods already created.

From where I stand now in the next parenting stage, my floors are still scattered with puzzle pieces and markers and Lego blocks, but the tiny baby onesies my girls once wore are currently dressing baby dolls. Our relationships are changing—my youngest is now seven, and my oldest is eleven and entering tween years. There's plenty of drama and big emotions and bickering, but even so, the things we've valued since they were little are still treasured. They are truly best friends (most of the time!). They love nature and beauty, shooting arrows and drawing princesses, sparkly things, and digging their hands in the dirt. With all the mistakes I've made in parenting, I'm glad I trusted my inner Mama Bear that roared against anything that tried to steal time from us or threaten their childhoods. Because it meant something.

My girls need me now in a different way than when they were tiny—not as much to care for their basic needs but to listen to their ideas, to encourage their natural talents, to simply spend time with them. Years later, I still keep returning to this truth: it's important to carve out a way of life for ourselves that allows for childhood—and time as a whole—to unravel slowly as the precious commodities they are.

But how?

A few years ago, I wrote my "Day in the Life" for a freelance writing project. The assignment was simply to record the ins and outs of an ordinary day in my life as a produce farmer, homeschool mom, and writer, from the moment I woke up to the moment my head hit the pillow again.

Although there aren't really any "ordinary" days out here, I chose a random weekday, which ended up being filled with a crazy conglomeration of things: from watering thousands of heads of lettuce in the greenhouse, to researching during school time about topics such as pottery makers in twelfth century Korea and why flamingoes have pink feathers, to making cinnamon toast, to reading library books at bedtime under the twinkle lights.

Through the process, I realized how many good and beautiful moments can be packed into, and unveiled by, our days amidst the inevitable struggles and challenges.

As much as I want to, I can't actually *stop* time. But in a way, *slowing down* time is in my control. This exercise showed me that the more I pay attention in the little moments—and also create opportunities for quality, purposeful time in relationship—the more I'm able to pull back the reins on time itself.

A new daily motto was unearthed, one that I try to abide by now as much as possible: *Today, I will log more moments in the present so time feels longer.*

I think of the days I've had that felt endless in the best possible way, like the weekend I delightfully misplaced my phone, and we spent all day Saturday and Sunday back at the cedar cabin in the woods cleaning and clearing out junk. The day stretched on without distraction. We spent hours and hours working side by side, getting dirty; we ate lunch while dangling our legs off the porch of the cabin, then collapsed exhausted in front of a campfire that evening. I didn't find my phone until the next morning under a chair outside covered in dew.

Or I remember many a weekend morning at our Dallas home when friends came over and we all cooked breakfast together, covering the farm table with every bowl and plate in the house. The coffee grinder got a run for its money as we ran it again and again to make more fresh pots. A stroll around the neighborhood turned into lunch, and we decided we might as well just keep it going as we raided the fridge for something we could make into dinner.

Or there are the school days when I'm able to release my tight grip on curricula and to-do lists long enough for us to be led by our interests. Somehow we end up chasing rabbit trails and fascinations, like learning about sloths or the muscular system or how diamonds form and how many carats are in the Crown Jewels of England—until it's suddenly 3:00 p.m., and we haven't even thought about lunch. These days aren't every day, but they are the ones that stand out, where we draw closer together in wonder and remember what we learned.

And then there was our one-year wedding anniversary trip, when we slowed down time with duct tape. Steven and I had the chance spend a week at a friend's family cabin in a remote town near Taos, New Mexico. I'd never been to New Mexico before, and it seemed like the perfect place to wear my favorite hippie-ish flowered skirt that Steven bought me at Urban Outfitters the year before on our honeymoon. I could barely wait to pack our hatchback car to the gills with yoga clothes, hiking shoes, and all the comfort foods we were planning to indulge in on vacation. The moment we entered the cabin, the rustic wood stove called to us, and the sound of the backyard creek rushed through the screened-in porch all the way into the kitchen.

We wanted to make the most of this. So we decided to do something we'd *never* done before: we covered all the clocks in the house with duct tape. We powered down our flip phones.

We decided we were going to have *no idea* what time it was for an entire week.

It felt so foreign at first. But soon, we started to fall into a new rhythm, listening to our bodies, souls, and instincts rather than expectations of what we *should* be doing at any particular hour of the day. Instead of letting time work against us, it was like a friend, unraveling slowly, measured not with numbers ticking by on a clock but with the way the sun shifted in the sky and the way the temperature felt on our skin.

That week, we observed hummingbirds at the feeders on the back porch for hours and took a million photos of them in midair. We ate giant bowls of vanilla-almond granola with whole milk whenever we wanted, not just at breakfast time. We dragged plastic chairs to the creek, set them right in the middle of it, and read books for hours with the water rushing around our toes. We stopped when we were hungry, hot, or tired. We lit candles and made dinner when it felt right.

With the lavishness of unmeasured time, we were able to stop and process the first year of our life together and remember the passions that brought us together in the first place. There was space for new conversations, depth, dreaming, a new level of relationship.

Of course, this was vacation. With both of us working full-time jobs in leadership positions, we didn't have the luxury of unmeasured time in our everyday lives. Who does?

But on that trip, just one year into marriage, something stirred in both of us, and we realized we couldn't afford not to at least build slower living moments into our normal lives whenever possible. An extra thirty minutes at breakfast on the stoop, lingering over toast and jam and creamy hot coffee. Leaving room on the weekends for inviting some single friends over to play Cranium until two thirty in the morning. We realized that something truly beautiful happens—an unparalleled level of connection—in those moments when we have the gift of time.

After one of our first Kindred Dinners here on the farm, a guest said the experience had given him "the chance to *slow down to the speed of listening*—to the stories of our food, to those gathered at the table, and to the larger conversation of community."

"Slow down to the speed of listening." I had never heard that phrase before. It stopped me in my tracks, and everything we'd been living and creating came into sharper focus.

We can't deny that time is a necessary ingredient for all living things, and slowing down is an essential part of how we're wired. No matter our personalities, we all need rest, breaks, quiet, and downtime.

But slowing down to the speed of listening is something altogether deeper. This is *slowing down with the purpose of connecting* with our families, our community, the flesh-and-blood people in our lives.

Slowing down to the speed of listening is an active, exciting, living, breathing experience. We must have moments of longer, uninterrupted time to provide space for conversations that go past the shallow waters into the depths. And not just at a special dinner on a farm or on a vacation, but the other 364 days a year.

And what happens when we slow down to the speed of listening? We find *perspective*. When we remove the dross, the things that are sucking our time that don't really matter, we're left with the gold. When we make time to hear another person's stories, we learn about how someone else sees the world. We have opportunities to grow our relationships. We learn more about the things that make us human in the first place.

I truly believe that slowing down to the speed of listening is possible for all of us, no matter who we are or where we live. Because some of the places I saw this most clearly were in remote villages of Kenya, Uganda, and India. The people there knew that relationship-driven, tightly knit, kindred living helps us survive—and that it's not a luxury but a necessity.

This isn't about privilege, wealth, or job status. This is about our humanity. This is about the need for visceral connection—to the people in our lives, to the land, to the food we eat—that is knitted into our very beings.

Somehow in our modern culture, we've lost this perspective. Busyness, frenzy, and chaos so often rule the day. So many of us are stressed, defined by online friendships rather than face-to-face ones, and feeling more disconnected than ever.

Wearing busyness like a badge of pride, we let our families, our homes, our relationships crumble under the weight of too much obligation and activities that don't have meaning. We're afraid of boredom, the imagination is stifled, and the natural world isn't interesting enough.

I know I've lost perspective again when I'm riddled with anxiety, unable to sleep, reaching for more screens and more stimulation. Before I know it, I'm scrolling on Instagram, unfazed, past photos that should be meaningful—like my friend's child's first day of school or spring flowers bursting from the ground on a hiking trail.

What on earth are we looking for?

We're looking for real connection. Fast, busy, and instant will never be enough for our souls. And it will never be enough for our relationships.

But we can't foster real connection in passing—in two minutes at a school pickup line, in the lobby at church, or in a quick business call. The speed of listening happens when you're *with* someone, not just *around* them or in the same room. We must carve out time for people, conversations, adventures, and meaningful experiences so we can live fully into who we were made to be.

Less pressure for "entertaining" or dinners that feel like a performance—more time in a messy kitchen with friends creating a simple meal together.

Less striving for perfection—more digging in the dirt, getting hands caked with flour, and breaking of the bread around our imperfect tables.

Less things that steal our time—more days where we lose sense of time.

Less busyness—more control over the precious minutes and hours.

Less isolation—more shared adventures.

Less digital—more analog.

Less scarcity—more abundance.

Less excuses—more action.

But be ready. Anytime we're reclaiming something and clearing space that's been choked out by weeds, there will be resistance.

There may be pushback from family members or even close friends who don't respect or understand our choices. There may be cracks and holes that need to be patched. There may be some hard nos that need to be said to get to the best yeses.

But we must keep fighting for what we know is true: one of the most valuable things we can offer other people is time to really see them. To hear them. And in the end, that wins.

In summer 2020, during the worldwide coronavirus pandemic, our oldest daughter turned ten, and our marriage turned fifteen. Our youngest lost her first tooth and learned to use a Hula-Hoop. My niece, whom I remember being born, graduated high school. Our girls grew so tall I did double takes.

When I looked back, among so much work and struggle, beautiful things were built and nurtured. It was the summer I went from wannabe flower farmer to flower farmer. I wrote thousands of hard-won words. We fought as a family to keep our businesses growing. There were bushels of crispy okra and moments spent lying in the corn rows with my girls at sunset. I grew my first garlic and onions and felt next-level Italian. There were sweat sessions in the greenhouse, where we cussed and begged for relief. There were new battle wounds: a half-moon shaped scar on one forearm and a burn mark on the other. There was artisan pizza on our new pizza oven. Lots and lots of pizza. There was lots of jam making, rainbow bouquets of wildflowers, blueberry picking, tree climbing, creek swimming.

It may seem like time is flying by, but really? There are a billion little moments that make up our days and seasons. It's not time that needs to slow down; it's *us*.

So I'll keep singing this rally cry for connection as long as there's breath in my lungs: it's time to recapture what's been lost—in our homes, our communities, and our relationships.

Wherever we live, whether we're farmers, musicians, assistants, executives, stay-at-home parents, accountants, teachers, or entrepreneurs, a different way of life—a kindred life—*is* possible.

If we can just slow down to the speed of listening, we might discover more about our communities, the people under our roofs, and who we were meant to be.

THIS CHAPTER IS ABOUT

savoring

We all want time to "slow down," but we rarely do anything about it. There are ways we can live so time feels slower, longer, and fuller of the things we truly value.

- Think of the moments that make you say out loud or to yourself, "Time, slow down!" What are those moments usually related to? What sparks that in you?

- Describe a day you can remember where time felt "endless" in a good way? Where were you? Who were you with? What did you do that day?

- What practices from that day can you build in your regular life, on a weekly basis, to stretch out time more and more?

- List some things you wish you had time for.

- What can you say no to that is stealing time away from you?

- What can you say yes to so you can log more moments in the present?

- Record your "day in the life" on an ordinary day. What do you notice about how you spend your time?

- Are you spending your time the way you want to?

Charcuterie Board with a Story

"This is an artistic expression of my love for you," Steven said. "You can open your eyes now."

On this July night of our fifteenth wedding anniversary, our girls were having a slumber party at a friend's house. This was the first night we'd ever spent in our home without them, and Steven and I were on the first date we'd had in months.

Laid out on the table before me was the most beautiful charcuterie board I'd ever seen, and with all the beautiful food I've seen him craft for his clients, that's really saying something.

This was food-turned-art that told a story: rainbows of color, uniqueness, different textures, flavors that complemented rather than competed . . . just like us.

Last summer's peach bourbon vanilla jam. Preserved figs, which always remind us of Texas. Pickled cauliflower we'd made earlier in the season. My favorite Cowgirl Creamery triple-cream brie. His favorite cheddar. Fresh tomatoes, cucumbers, hot peppers, and a few leaves of lemon basil—all straight from our farm, all grown from seed in midwinter. A wooden jam spoon our neighbor Jessica had hand-carved from one of our fallen trees after an epic spring storm. Rainbow carrots, which are on our farm logo even though we can't grow them well yet because it takes years to nourish the soil and build up the layers.

All of this was carefully arranged by a self-trained chef who loves experimenting with flavor and whose creativity and love are expressed through food. Enjoyed by me, a woman who probably wouldn't have eaten most of this stuff fifteen years ago but has now found a lot more food freedom.

One shared meal savored over hours on the land we've worked together with our family, celebrating a marriage we've fought hard for.

In the artisan food world, things that take more time are more valuable in general. The older bourbon. The long-aged cheese. The heirloom tomato sauce recipe that takes days to simmer and has been passed down for generations.

A charcuterie board is one of the best shared food experiences that encourages the slow unraveling of time.

It has a feeling of a special feast, without anyone having to cook a thing. You don't even need plates. From a common plate or board in the middle of the table, you're anchored in your time together, in your nourishment.

Here's how to build your own. Have at least two varieties in each of these categories:

- meat
- cheese
- pickled items

- jam
- hummus
- fruit

- nuts
- something sweet,
  like chocolate

Within each category, make the varieties different. For example:

- hard cheese and a soft cheese
- plain salami and a spicy salami
- pickled spicy okra and olives stuffed with cheese
- marcona almonds and candied pecans

Add unusual, fun things, such as unique potato chips, queso or cashew cheese, corn nuts.

As you select your elements, can you add any items that symbolize a memory or tell a story about the people who will be sharing the charcuterie board?

Use a wooden cutting board to display everything. To assemble, start with your cheese and make small groupings in different spots on the board. Then take your next item, like meat, and make small groupings next to the cheese. The goal is to not have all of one item in the same spot.

Assembling a board takes a while, and it takes care. This is a great thing to do with someone who will be at the table with you.

Put dips and nuts in small bowls and put those on the board. Then display cheeses and fruits around the bowls.

Cover the entire board space—"Always crowd the board." (I learned this from Steven.)

Set your board in the middle of the table where you'll be sitting or in a living room on a coffee table, where you can be comfortable for a while. The point isn't walking up to a table, grabbing a cracker and some cheese, and walking away, but setting up space for people to linger, to see one another across the table, to connect.

"

Only by **restoring the**
broken connections
can we be healed. Connection is health. . . .
We lose our health . . . by failing to see
the direct connections between
living and eating, eating and
working, working and loving.

—WENDELL BERRY,
THE ART OF THE COMMONPLACE

CHAPTER 14

The Table Is for Everyone

I f you encountered anyone in my big Italian American New Jersey family growing up, they would probably adopt you or, at the very least, set a place for you at the dinner table and ask you to stay all weekend. Because that's just what they do.

My first cousin Paula, her husband, Steve, and her three children all lived just a few towns over from where I grew up in Madison, New Jersey. My dad's sister, Aunt Lucille, lived with them too. After a short ten-minute drive through suburbia, we'd pull into their driveway, which always seemed to be crammed with cars at all hours of the day and night.

I'd open the screen door on the long, covered front porch and feel myself exhale as I walked into their inviting home, which was an open door to welcome friends, their kids' friends, relatives, and neighbors. It was a place where I felt immediately known.

On birthdays, at Communion parties, and on every major holiday, we would feast like there was no tomorrow. It began with Aunt Lucille's tomato sauce simmering for hours, which she would then use to make baked ziti. I can remember that smell now of walking in the house. Everyone was there, from the babies up to the elderly, and the house was *loud*.

So many people showed up for dinner that Paula and Steve had to use the leaf to extend the length of their already long dining room table and add a couple of card tables at the end.

Sitting around this long makeshift table for hours—eating inordinate amounts of homemade Italian food, laughing, and attempting to talk over everyone at high decibels—has always been one of my favorite things.

After Steven and I had been dating for seven months, I took him home to New Jersey to meet my family. We took the New Jersey Transit train into New York City for the day (just a quick forty-five-minute ride from my hometown). On a cool December afternoon on a hill carpeted with bright-yellow leaves, he handed me a blank leather book with some crayon drawings he'd made of big moments so far in our relationship. I flipped through the book, delighted, and came to a blank page. Into my palms he placed a small wooden box containing a bundle of crayons tied together with a long string. When I picked up the crayons, something clinked on the side of the box, and I realized it was an engagement ring! I gasped. He got down on one knee and asked if I would continue to fill up the pages with him for the rest of my life.

A few days later, as we were about to take our first bites of braciola around Aunt Lucille's table, Steven raised a glass of Prosecco and declared nervously in front of the entire Italian family (who he knew had my back through thick or thin), "I have an announcement!" As if the group could get any louder or merrier, the celebration heightened when they realized another person was being added to the fold.

Every time we visited New Jersey after that, it was just a given that we'd gather for another huge family dinner at Paula's house—first the salad, then the grilled meat and eggplant, and then all of a sudden, out come the peaches slathered in honey and sprinkled with almonds. Hers was a full Italian spread with an antipasto platter, bubbling homemade sauce and meatballs, lasagna, eggplant parmigiana, Aunt Lucille's pillowy-soft ricotta cookies and cannoli for dessert, and after, espresso with a twist of lemon or coffee with generous shots of Sambuca.

Every bite, every taste, was amazing. At the end of a meal, it seems we always had about a vat of baked ziti left over, even after a bazillion people ate as much as they could. But that's okay, because the only thing better than baked ziti is baked ziti on day two, three, four . . .

My family injected love into their dishes. It made me feel special to be cooked for, to be fussed over, and to be fed their very best—carefully prepared, delicious comfort food.

But ultimately, it wasn't the food that was important. It was the preparation, the welcoming, the inclusion that made me feel special and known. Not until I grew up and had my own home and traditions did I realize how much this family table of abundance was woven into my story.

In my childhood home in New Jersey, some of our best Thanksgiving holidays were those where people we barely knew from the community accepted my mom's invitation to join us. In our carpeted dining room, the ornate cherry wood dining table, usually covered with mail and random odds and ends, was cleared off and shined with lemon furniture polish. The Thanksgiving table was opened to anyone my mom would meet at church or the grocery store or just in town.

"Do you have anywhere to go for Thanksgiving?" she would ask. If they said no, she would invite them without stipulation. And most Thanksgivings, several new friends showed up, like a single older lady my mom met at the pool or one of my internet friends who had just moved to New York City.

While the turkey was roasting in its brown-in bag, we crammed into the living room and watched snippets of the Macy's Thanksgiving Day Parade, knowing the whole magical thing was happening just thirty miles away from us in "the City." My grandfather, who used to be an elevator operator at Rockefeller Center, would never miss the performance by "his girls," the Rockettes.

When dinner was finally ready and the smell of turkey gravy, candied sweet potatoes, and roasted pearl onions (my grandfather's favorites) had perfumed every inch of my parents' little Tudor cottage, we added chairs and all rubbed elbows while reaching for spoonfuls of buttered veggies, stuffing, and cranberry sauce (the gelatinous kind from the can). After dinner, we served up generous slices of pie: Dutch apple, mince, or coconut custard.

We welcomed people into our small, humble home and family traditions. I have to admit that as a moody preteen, the extra guests made me feel uncomfortable at first—I didn't want to talk to *anyone*, much less strangers around our table. But now, creating space for belonging around the table is one of my favorite things my mom has taught me. Once we sat down around that table, it just felt right.

Before I met Steven, I had a huge group of single friends (except for Jeremy and Shannon, our one token married couple), a mix of guys and girls, and we did everything together. Beach trips to Destin, Florida, hanging out on the weekends listening to one of our many musician friends play guitar, sand volleyball games at the park.

One year as Valentine's Day was approaching, my old roommate Suz and I decided to do something special so none of us singles would feel left out. We decided to have a dinner that we called "Here's to Love" at our little rental house. I had met Steven at the conference in Branson, Missouri, the month before, but we'd gone our separate ways and hadn't started talking regularly yet. I had no idea what the future would hold.

Suz made her family's recipe for cinnamon rolls, I made the invitations, and we drove around town putting paper plates of treats with the invites on our friends' doorsteps. A few days later, on Valentine's night, we put together *all* the tables and chairs we had to form one long table down the center of our living room.

I made the only things I really knew to make—Aunt Lucille's lasagna and her spaghetti and meatballs. There was even a "tulip ceremony" and a dance party. It was patched together and wonderful, full of love, friendship, camaraderie.

In our home with the yellow door in Dallas, the scent of garlic and the sound of forks clinking on plates were permanently infused into the walls from all the meals we not only ate but prepared together as well. Around our beloved, weathered eight-foot dining table that Steven built himself with salvaged barn wood, milestones were celebrated, babies were cradled, glasses were filled and refilled, and tear-filled and joyous conversations were shared.

When we decided we were moving to Tennessee, we sat around that table making plans, trying to work out the dizzying details, wondering what would happen next.

Since we didn't know where we were going to end up once we moved, we had to get rid of a lot of belongings like that beloved table, which was so heavy that it had to be disassembled to be moved. I can still remember every knot and divot in that table and imagine where I was sitting in different pivotal or just ordinary moments. Toddler Luci would crawl underneath it and stick her chubby little finger through a knothole while I was drinking morning tea. Both my babies had their high chairs scooted up next to it so they could be a part of the action. I can see dear friends like Michelle and Kyle smiling across the table at me at one of our many meals shared around it—with fresh corn or beans that Michelle brought from the farmers market, or crostini with Pecorino and wine that Kyle had brought back from one of her trips to Italy.

We gave the table to our close friends Tommy and Linda, who took it home in pieces. They had also joined us around it countless times; we knew they would appreciate it and use it to nourish others.

While we were renting a small home in the country before we moved to the farm, our dining room was empty. Out of the blue, my dear college friend Angela asked, "Hey, any chance you need a wooden table for six? My office is getting rid of one." I scurried over to her office faster than you could imagine and loaded it into the back of our Tahoe.

I'll be ever thankful to Ange for that because the sweet little table was a physical anchor through a season of so much transition. It ended up being the centerpiece of our dining room for *four more years* in our Kindred farmhouse.

All during those four years, I dreamed of knocking out a wall in our dining room so we could re-create the table we left behind in Dallas.

But this hand-me-down one was special too. It was just big enough for our family and a few guests (if you squeezed in and added chairs on the corners). There were scratches and pen marks my toddler made when I wasn't looking. There were for sure sticky smoothie drippings on the surface. And the memories shared around its edges were numerous—Christmas night dinner of boeuf bourguignon, homemade bread, and peppermint chocolate cake with friends who, like us, didn't have any family in town. Wine and homemade pasta with my parents visiting from New Jersey. Homemade kimchi and rice and Korean barbecue, which we cooked on a propane grill set in the middle of the table, with Steven's parents visiting from Texas. Easter brunch of crisp salad and potato latkes with seventy-seven-degree sunshine streaming in the window.

That table is where we sat and dreamed about what Kindred could be and then started putting legs to those dreams. We always knew that little table would be temporary—we just didn't know "temporary" would be four years.

I hoped to eventually move it into the school room to give us more work and craft space. I also hoped to build a new farm table for the dining room that would stand the test of time and witness countless more meals and memories.

And then, on a January day, we decided to do it.

Steven and I went out to the barn. I pointed to five weathered boards of old wood from an unfinished section on an inside wall and told Steven, "I want those." He removed them with a crowbar.

For three days, we hammered, drilled, sanded, painted. After the last layer of clear topcoat had dried, the new table was finally done.

It not only holds eight to ten people comfortably but also already had a story before we ever sat around it. All four of us signed our names underneath the boards in Sharpie, permanently inscribing the story of how it was built:

- The boards were salvaged from the inside of our barn.
- The frame was made from leftover wood our friends gave us from their newly built house.
- The legs were cut from posts we used to string lights at our Kindred Dinners.
- And the white paint for the legs came from a can of paint we were saving in our basement for a bunk-bed project that never was.

There are so many imperfections and textures that give the table character: a board that's slightly sloped, small gaps between boards where game pieces could get stuck, and a triangle piece missing at one end where you could, conveniently, scrape all the crumbs to the floor.

There's even a knot that has a little heart in the middle. Because of course.

We moved it into the dining room, arms trembling from trying to steadily hold the hundred-plus pounds of solid wood. It barely fit through the doorways of our house, and we had to move the couch out of the way in the living room to swing it wide enough to get it into the dining room. Our girls were scattering left and right, trying to move things out of the way so Steven and I had a clear path.

And then we set it down, right under the one window that looks out onto the side yard with the loblolly pine trees, the Forest of Fun, and Fairy Creek.

It fit perfectly.

In an instant, it seemed like it had always been there. I was absolutely giddy, jumping up and down like a five-year-old and hugging my incredible husband, who had set aside all other seemingly bigger priorities in our lives for those three days to handcraft this piece of beauty.

This new table speaks of our backstory together—the family culture we built together in another home in another state—while also telling our new story as a family in Tennessee.

On a warm October evening, eleven long tables were set end to end to form one big, long table down the center of a meadow, and twinkle lights were draped overhead. Dressed in white tablecloths, mismatched fabric napkins, clear glass plates, flickering candles and lanterns, and magenta and orange wildflowers in turquoise mason jars, the table shined like a beacon as dusk started to settle on the Tennessee hillside. This table said, *Relax. Exhale. Savor. I've prepared a place for you.*

A songwriter played guitar in the background. In the pasture nearby, without any electricity, chefs created a makeshift kitchen using fire and steel grates and grills. Over these burning coals, they cooked the finest seasonal, farm-fresh fare: fire-roasted squash, potatoes, and beans; fresh bread and desserts; homemade pasta with Bolognese sauce; and porchetta from pastured pork that had been happily raised in the adjacent pasture.

As this fresh, rich meal was being carefully prepared, almost a hundred dinner guests slowly began arriving. Everyone was chattering excitedly; no one was in a hurry. As they passed over the crest of the hill encircled by blazing autumn trees flickering at the edge of the forest, they saw the long table set for them, waiting for them, and their eyes widened.

Each person chose a seat with friends they already knew—or perhaps, they were brave to sit next to someone new. They mingled and talked and awaited the first course, and soon, wooden salad bowls were placed before them piled high with buttery lettuce grown in the field just down the hill.

This scene was actually real: it was our first farm-to-table dinner on Kindred Farm in October 2017, a night of gathering both old and new friends on our own farm at a long table under the stars and twinkle lights. A dream literally years in the making, all the way back to the first tables where I was welcomed and learned to welcome others.

Before we even got to the feasting part, the behind-the-scenes preparation and anticipation of gathering around the table brought unity and camaraderie. Every friend, farmer, chef, and artisan involved in the event offered up their gifts and abilities, and with each person doing his or her part, things went smoothly. Well, as smoothly as things can go for a first-time dinner for a hundred people in the middle of a pasture when you've never actually done this before.

Our close friend Amy offered her time and expertise as our event producer, bringing her unique talents to keep things running smoothly and considering all the important details that bring delight and wonder.

Others hustled to finish constructing our barn, paint a mural on the side, hang signs, and cut tree stumps to hold lanterns to light the path at night.

Our photographer/farmer neighbor, Sarah, grew and picked the wildflowers that would dress our tables and agreed to capture photos during the evening so we could sear it into our memories. For the bonfires and cooking fires, her husband, Patrick, delivered trucks of firewood from his own woodlot, selecting the most fragrant varieties so you could walk past the fire and smell the sweet, perfumy scent perfectly intermingled with the savory smell of food. The chefs spent hours developing and collaborating and prepping an exquisite menu.

Even so, in true Christine style, I had been nervous about the unknowns and unpredictability. *Are we really welcoming people we don't know to a dinner on our land just steps away from our house? Will this feel invasive? Will it go smoothly? Will they go home happy?* These people were purchasing tickets and trusting we would deliver.

But Steven and I, with an incredible team surrounding us, pushed through challenges and walked forward with the clear vision God has given our family to gather people around the table to slow down and connect on this beautiful land that's been entrusted to us.

Some people arrived at the dinner as strangers, but by the end of the night, they were sharing stories of their lives, exchanging texts, and making plans to see one another again.

By spring 2019, many dinners later, we'd still had a perfect weather track record. On the scheduled evening of our spring dinner, the rain was finally coming. For days, we checked the weather apps obsessively until the moment we realized the storms were inevitable. I had crippling anxiety over how it would all unfold, not wanting to disappoint the guests who were paying for and expecting a wonderful experience.

The team went to work. With the help of so many hands, including both of Steven's parents who were visiting from Texas, we moved machinery and equipment, dug trenches for water to be rerouted, and transformed our greenhouse, a place that had been covered in dirt forty-eight hours before, into a twinkle-lit room where more than a hundred guests would be welcomed, loved, and served.

At dinnertime, the guests showed up with cheerful attitudes in the rain, with their rain boots and umbrellas, entrusting us with their evening, their time, and their hunger.

As the night went on, all of us saw something extra special unfold: the level of connection was greater than we'd *ever* seen before at our dinners—the shared stories, the strangers becoming friends, the camaraderie.

In my shallow vision, I thought our best-case scenario was that it wouldn't rain, but instead God wanted to show me—and so many others—how beautiful and intimate and nourishing breaking bread together can be in the very midst of a storm.

We'll never forget this night and what it taught us: no matter the weather, any setting can become a sacred space of connection with the willing hearts of those who are there.

And that's the beauty of what can happen around the table. It's more than a piece of furniture; it's a place where our bodies and souls are nourished.

Many more big Kindred Dinners and several years later, it still doesn't get old seeing people connect on a deep level as they walk around the farm, clink their glasses, linger at the table, and huddle around a roaring fire.

I hope that anyone who comes to dinner on our farm sees that this is never a performance. We make it beautiful and lovely and magical because *we care about the people coming*, and we want to prepare a place for them. I hope the heart behind it is always what shines through and people feel like they belong.

Our friend Amy, who was the producer for our first Kindred Dinners, once told me, "In the world we know today, true hospitality is rebellious, radical. The act of opening yourself up to give or receive a meal, a drink, or a safe place to stay, flies in the face of a culture fixated on speed and self-reliance. To willingly place yourself in the hands of another, and exchange feelings of welcome and gratitude, may well be the ancient practice that keeps saving us."

The other crucial flip side of hospitality? The act of showing up and being willing to be fed. It's one of the ultimate acts of vulnerability.

Every time I look over that sea of wide-eyed people (up to 150 guests now!), I see a glimpse of all the life-filled tables of my journey—the big Italian family dinners, the cozy Thanksgivings, the gatherings with single friends, the ones in our urban Dallas home, the first farm dinner in a city brewery. And I realize they're all singing the same anthem: *The table is for everyone.*

There's something about gathering around a physical table that unites us. No matter who you are, where you're from, or where you live, feasting together is something human beings were meant to do.

The book of Psalms in the Bible compares the deep soul nourishment of salvation to the ultimate feast, the ultimate food and drink.

There will be another table, one that will be filled with every single person I know and love, and it will go on as far as the eye can see.

The feast will stretch on for hours, and no one will have any food intolerances or restrictions. We will never be full. Our souls will be satisfied in a way we could not even fathom now if we tried.

I believe that one day, it'll happen.

> In Jerusalem, the Lord of Heaven's Armies
> > will spread a wonderful feast
> > for all the people of the world.
> It will be a delicious banquet
> > with clear, well-aged wine and choice meat.
> There he will remove the cloud of gloom,
> > the shadow of death that hangs over the earth.
> He will swallow up death forever!
> > The Sovereign Lord will wipe away all tears.[1]

I believe this will be a real feast, but whether or not you do, too, can you believe, just for a moment, that we can all do our part to stop the cycle of busyness and rushing and chaos to create sacred space around the tables in our homes?

We have a chance to create a refuge like that—right here and now. You can do something to redeem the earth, little by little, by creating space in your home to nourish people's bodies and souls.

Please, don't let the striving for perfection—perfect food, perfect setting, perfect timing—stop you from inviting people in.

I almost learned this the hard way back in Dallas when I panicked before having friends over for dinner one night. I was feeling uncomfortable in my skin and clothes, like I was taking up too much space in the world again. The bad-body-image tape was replaying in my head on loop. Somewhere in the middle of preparing this fun meal for my friends and acquaintances, who were soon to be arriving, I neglected what is perhaps the most important part: *there's room at the table for me too.*

I pushed through, reminding myself that people don't want to be entertained. They want to feel welcomed and known. And I couldn't do that if I was focusing on my own insecurities.

I chose to be vulnerable.

I chose to open the door.

And I chose to share a meal with people.

When the night ended, I realized that what made it special and memorable had nothing to do with how my clothes fit and everything to do with showing up with my authentic self. What an honor and privilege we have every time someone gathers around our table to offer our own vulnerability and meet them in theirs.

The table matters because people matter.

The table is where we gather, where we come to sacred, common ground, where we laugh around board games and scoot in extra chairs to welcome guests. It's where all the little elements of our daily, beautifully ordinary lives are scattered: colored pencils, random drinking glasses (always way more than there are people in the house), drawings, notebooks, walkie-talkies, puzzle pieces.

What kind of table doesn't matter—only that there is a physical, grounding piece of furniture that unites us in our humanity. Around it, we meet our needs for connection and sustenance. At that table, however scarred it may be, we are anchored through seasons of transition and are able to create safe, stable spaces for others.

I'm so glad we haven't waited for the "perfect" table to invite people into our normal, messy lives the last four years. Because no one really cares if a table is brand-new and fancy or a scratched, sticky hand-me-down—they just want to be welcomed in.

THIS CHAPTER IS ABOUT

belonging

The table is more than a piece of furniture; it's a place where our bodies and souls are nourished. I've described many (but not all!) of the significant tables of my life where love and nourishment and connection have drawn me back time and again.

- What are the significant tables of your life, and what are some memorable moments that have happened there?

- Have you ever had an experience where you felt too insecure to welcome someone into your home and around your table? What do you think you might have missed out on?

- How can you invite people in around your table now, as is, however messy or imperfect? Name three possible ways and choose the one you'll pursue first.

Kindred Farm Salad

One of my absolute favorite things? Picking dinner. Are you even a farmer if, at some point, you haven't harvested something, strapped it in, and let it ride shotgun in the truck back to the house?

The primary crop we grow on Kindred Farm year-round is a type of lettuce called "salanova," which comes in eight different leaf shapes and two colors: green and red. When it's growing down a one-hundred-foot row, densely planted, it looks like a one-hundred-foot purple-and-green carpet. When we harvest it, we remove the leaves from the core and mix it all together to create our Buttery Sweet Salad Mix.

For this recipe, any fresh, fluffy lettuce will do. A spring mix would be perfect, or romaine mixed with butter lettuce. Anything but iceberg! Of course, you can purchase the lettuce at the grocery store, but I encourage getting some from your local farmer, if possible. Also, lettuce is super easy to grow in early spring, if you want to give it a try, and few things are more delicious than a crunchy salad made with lettuce that was in the ground, pulsing with life, thirty minutes ago.

I always, always, always have a big bowl of salad as the centerpiece of any dinner, especially when we have other people over. And it's a great thing to build together with a friend in the kitchen.

"How do you know what to put in it to make it taste like this?" they say. Well, here ya go! I never follow a "recipe" for salad. It's more a formula for elements that, when put together, make for an interesting salad with a balance of textures and flavors.

Makes as many servings as you need

Foundation
1/2 cup lettuce per person

Veggies (choose any or all)

Thinly sliced cucumbers

Carrots peeled into long ribbons

Halved cherry tomatoes

Thinly sliced celery

Sliced bell peppers or sweet peppers

Halved garlic-stuffed green olives

Grated raw beets

Sliced radishes

Broccoli or cauliflower florets, finely chopped

Creamy (choose 1)

Crumbled goat cheese

Crumbled feta cheese

Raw Parmesan cheese peeled into
shavings

Crunchy (choose 1 or 2)

Sunflower seeds

Honey-toasted cashews

Toasted almonds

Toasted pecans

Toasted walnuts

Sweet (choose 1)

Pitted dates, chopped (my favorite!)

Raisins

Dried figs

Dried apricots

Finishing touches (choose 1 or 2)

Sprinkle of nutritional yeast (which
our family calls "cheesy flakes"—
great for a nondairy option!)

Sprinkle of hemp seeds

Sprinkle of garlic powder (Aunt
Lucille's secret ingredient)

Edible flowers: purple pea flowers
are our favorite, but you can
also use calendula flower petals,
marigolds, pansies, dandelions, and
nasturtiums (just be 100 percent
sure you're selecting edible flowers
that haven't been sprayed with
chemicals)

Start with the foundation, and then add all the extras. I can't give you exact measurements for these, but I can tell you that as you add them, you'll want to either put each element in a tight pile and then pile the next thing next to it, or evenly place each item over the surface of your bed of lettuce. When you're done adding toppings, the entire top of your bowl should be covered, without any lettuce showing. When you toss it with the dressing, it'll come together like magic.

NOTES

- To make honey-toasted cashews, preheat the oven to 350 degrees. Spread raw cashews on a large rimmed baking sheet, place it in the oven, and toast the cashews for 5 to 10 minutes, until they're golden brown. Stay nearby though—they toast quickly! After you remove them from the oven, immediately drizzle raw honey on top and toss; then sprinkle with sea salt.

- Alternatively, you can toast the cashews in a dry pan over medium heat for a few minutes until golden brown. Drizzle raw honey on top and toss, sprinkle with sea salt, and remove from the pan.

Go-To Vinaigrette

This is my standard vinaigrette. I always have a big glass jar of it ready to go, stored with a tight lid in my spice pantry. Because when you're making a salad for dinner, you don't want to have to whip up a new batch of dressing every single time.

Makes approximately 4 servings

1 cup extra virgin olive oil
$1/3$ to $1/2$ cup acid (see suggestions below)
3 to 4 tablespoons Dijon mustard
Big pinch of sea salt to taste
Cracked black pepper to taste

In a large jar with a lid, combine the olive oil, acid, mustard, sea salt, and pepper.

Close the lid tightly and shake hard! Shake until the Dijon blends in well, there are no lumps, and the dressing looks blended and creamy.

Alternatively, you could put all of it in a blender and whizz it up, then pour any extra into a jar to store.

NOTES

- My go-to acid is apple cider vinegar, but other great choices are balsamic vinegar, fresh lemon juice, champagne vinegar, and red wine vinegar. The amount you add to the dressing determines whether it's milder or tangier.
- It's hard to overdo the Dijon mustard, which gives the dressing extra tang and the perfect creaminess.

Kindred Farm Honey-Basil Balsamic Vinaigrette

Perfect for summer, when you have lots of extra basil! This is best made fresh for each salad or made in a bigger batch and refrigerated so you can use it in a few days.

Makes 2 servings

6 tablespoons extra virgin olive oil

2 tablespoons balsamic vinegar

2 tablespoon Dijon mustard

2 tablespoons raw honey

8 to 10 fresh basil leaves

Sea salt to taste

Cracked black pepper to taste

In a blender, place the olive oil, vinegar, mustard, honey, basil, salt, and pepper.

Blend on high for about 10 seconds, until creamy.

Taste and adjust salt and pepper to your preference.

Pour over salad and toss lightly.

Aunt Lucille's Ricotta Cookies

The sound of laughter and the smell of marinara sauce and meatballs filled the entryway of the house on Kinney Street. The December air outside was chilly in New Jersey. Bundled in a wool coat and boots, a four-year-old little girl climbed the tunnel-like steps to the second-floor apartment of her aunt Lucille and uncle Tony. Her feet could barely reach above each stair, but the comforting aroma led her quickly into the warm home.

It was Christmas afternoon, and about twenty people were already crammed into the tiny kitchen and around the dining room table, which was the centerpiece of the family. It was the site of classic Italian American meals of baked ziti, homemade meatballs, braciola, and garlicky salad with black olives (and that was just the first course), along with every dessert you could possibly imagine.

Before dinner, the little girl's favorite thing to do was put a black olive on each finger and call them "meatballs." Her favorite dessert was the ricotta cookies with tiny rainbow sprinkles. After dessert, the dining room erupted into a game of Pokeno or long conversation over unmarked bottles of red wine.

These are some of my most vivid childhood memories with my Italian family. The kids were always included in the fold, crammed into the tiny dining room with everyone else, allowed to help in the kitchen and be involved in the family recipes. Aunt Lucille's table was one of the places I felt the most welcomed in the world. When she passed away from lung cancer at only sixty-nine years old, just a month before I got pregnant with my first daughter, it was one of the saddest things I've ever experienced. But I take her heritage with me to this day, in the life I live with my family around the table. I wish she were still here, but I know she'd be proud to share this recipe, one of her best, with you.

Makes approximately 2 dozen cookies

For the cookies
1/2 cup butter, softened

1/4 cup whole milk ricotta cheese

1 teaspoon vanilla

1 cup sugar

1 egg

2 cups flour

1/2 teaspoon baking soda

1/2 teaspoon salt

For the frosting
1 1/2 cups powdered sugar

1 teaspoon vanilla

A few teaspoons whole milk

Tiny, round white or rainbow sprinkles

Preheat the oven to 350 degrees.

In a stand mixer, blend the softened butter with the ricotta cheese.

Add the vanilla, sugar, and egg to the butter and cheese mixture, and blend until smooth.

In a medium bowl, combine the flour, baking soda, and salt.

Add the dry ingredients to the wet ingredients in the stand mixer bowl and blend until smooth.

Roll the dough into balls about 1.5 inches wide, and space them evenly on a large cookie sheet lined with parchment paper (or a greased cookie sheet if you don't have parchment paper).

Bake the cookies for 10 to 12 minutes.

While the cookies bake, make the frosting by mixing the powdered sugar, vanilla, and milk together in a medium bowl and whisking until smooth. Add enough milk so the mixture isn't too runny but is able to be easily drizzled over the cookies.

Remove the cookies from the oven and let them cool on a cookie sheet. After they cool, drizzle frosting over each one and then cover with round white or rainbow sprinkles.

"

The second journey begins when we know we

cannot live the afternoon of life according

to the morning program. We are aware that

we only have a limited

amount of time left

to accomplish that which is really important—

and that awareness illumines for us what

really matters, what really counts.

—BRENNAN MANNING,
THE RAGAMUFFIN GOSPEL

CHAPTER 15

It's Not Too Late

In farming, you can miss the window. It can definitely be too late for us to plant the sunflowers so they bloom in time for the fall farm dinner. It can be too late to sow the pea cover crop in time to add nutrients back into the soil before the frost. It can be too late to rescue the radishes that have been choked out by weeds.

But with ourselves? *It's never too late.*

I wish I could talk to my early twenties self, the girl I was when this journey began—before I boarded a solo plane to India, before I held orphans on my lap in Uganda, before I grew a garden and tended it in my red Crocs with babies by my side, before I became a farmer, before I began to embrace change.

She might not believe me if I told her that one day she'd be standing on the land she's farmed wearing worn leather boots and new lines on her face that tell stories. I'd tell her: There will be blunders. You'll make big mistakes and have moments where you feel like you're falling apart. You'll miss pieces of your old life. But you'll find your strength in new ways. You'll gain a sky above your house that's an actual planetarium. A connection to the land that is palpable. Space for people to come and slow down and connect over farm-fresh meals or a campfire. A marriage that's grown through struggle. And two girls who will one day help you plant wildflowers and lie on the ground among the corn rows with you at golden hour.

I'd tell her: The good things you've always been haven't changed. You're still the same girl who will never pass up an opportunity to blow dandelion seeds into the air (sorry, perfectly manicured lawns). You like wearing sparkly paper crowns at your daughter's birthday party and playing catch and climbing trees and jumping off the diving board and swimming in waterfalls.

You still believe in the healing power of God through nature and beauty and adventure. You're still the playful, young-at-heart girl you've always been, just more seasoned, with a few more gray hairs and wrinkles, of course.

I'd tell her that all the small steps forward weren't small at all, and they mattered. I'd tell her that there's still so much more to do, but she'll be proud of how far she's come.

Last September, the one hundred feet of zinnias I planted in April were being completely taken over by weeds. I went out there early and wild-haired one morning and started ripping the weeds out, and I realized that with every weed I pulled, I was saying under my breath, "Reclaim. Reclaim, reclaim, reclaim."

Reclaim means that there is something that needs to be brought back under cultivation, something that is under our stewardship, given to us by God. Peace. Freedom. Joy. The honor and privilege of planting and growing and beautifying. There are no "too small" acts of reclamation. Every bit matters and counts.

I knew that day that reclaiming the zinnias was about much more than weeds. Sometimes there are things we have to undo. We may feel the consequences of letting things go too far for too long. Those runners and weeds got so bad that they completely covered the landscape fabric walking path that I had laid down. *I could no longer see the path.*

It's time to reclaim it now—whatever "it" is. Boundary lines around your family's time. Your children's childhood. Your own voice. Your calling. The dirt in your own backyard. Your bedroom as a haven. Your health. Your home and your table as a place of peace and connection.

Rip. It. Out.

Your plants will breathe again.

You will breathe again.

Remember at the beginning when I told you about Doc, the pastor who married Steven and me in the rain and taught us about our separate Hula-Hoops? Here's another thing he taught me: freedom isn't the same as a "free-for-all." Freedom isn't the *absence* of limitations; it is the *choice* of limitations.

As humans with God-given agency, we have the ability to design our own program for freedom in our lives. And that will take making some choices: What fits and what no longer fits? What will we need to rip out and plant anew? And will we be willing to see the beauty that's found not just on the other side but also in the messy middle?

It may all seem hard, but I'm here to tell you are made up of "the stuff" it takes to get there. Because we don't want perfection; we want real. You have a voice. You have a song to sing that's uniquely yours.

You have a special way of seeing this world, and we need you to bring it to our world.

To grow, you will have to push yourself in new ways and be uncomfortable. But on the other side? You might discover you're the you-est you've ever been. More weathered? Yes, but exquisitely so.

The soil doesn't lie; the actual ground beneath our feet here on Kindred Farm is different now than it was five years ago. If we nourish the land or our relationships or our souls with the right things, they *will* change and transform with time. They will become healthier and grow more abundant things.

Wherever you've come from,

whatever your talents,

wherever you live,

whatever you've lived through,

whatever you have or haven't accomplished in this life,

as long as you're here, living and breathing, *it's not too late.*

Kindred is about relationship. It's about inviting people in, now. It's that feeling of being part of a family or tribe that's as ancient as time itself, that we all deeply want and need.

We can find it in the soil, in community, and around the table. In a suburban neighborhood, a city parking lot, an urban backyard, a slum in Kenya, a concrete church in India, a random conference hall in Missouri, on Texas land, and in the grittiest, toughest moments on a farm in Tennessee.

You don't need a curated home or perfect family. You don't have to be introverted or extroverted or "good at cooking" or have a green thumb to live a rich, nourishing life of connection. You just have to be willing to show up and dig in.

And friend, I don't want you to wait any longer. Because no matter what I've written in this book, you won't experience "kindred" until you touch it, taste it, feel it for yourself.

The Kindred Life *is* worth fighting for. Whatever we're doing to nourish something in our lives—a garden, a calling, a family, a dream—changing and transforming and reclaiming won't be easy, but the richness of what is grown in that soil is so, *so* worth it.

The fact that deep connection and true, staggering beauty is created out of the dirt and mess is a lesson I keep learning over and over again.

Will you join me?

Let's walk forward, singing our uniquely gorgeous, gritty songs together. We haven't missed the window. *It's not too late.*

THIS LAST CHAPTER IS ABOUT

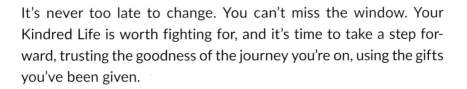

It's never too late to change. You can't miss the window. Your Kindred Life is worth fighting for, and it's time to take a step forward, trusting the goodness of the journey you're on, using the gifts you've been given.

- Write a letter to your past self. What do you wish you could say? What wisdom do you have now, from where you stand today? What can you see from the journey that has unfolded?
- What is something deeply rooted inside you that wants to be expressed?
- What about your life do you wish to change? What are you going to do about it?
- What are things you've always been?
- What are things you've always loved?
- How can you reconnect with them now?
- Spend some time thinking about the gifts you have to offer the world. How will you make the choice to offer them up, to sing your song?
- What have you learned about living a life of deeper purpose and connection?
- Who is a trusted person (or who are trusted people) on this journey with you?
- What is *your* Kindred Life?

CHAPTER 16

Your Own Kindred Dinner

I don't want you to wait another minute to start inviting people in. So here's a little guide to make it easier for you to start connecting with people around the table.

One of the biggest misconceptions people have about opening up their homes is that you're the host and everything has to be perfectly prepared before the "guests" arrive. This is understandably intimidating and can easily fall into the feeling of a performance. This isn't the way of kindred. Kindred is about simple gathering in an imperfect yet authentic way. Here's the difference between entertaining and simple gathering: when you work on something *together*. Kindred says that it's always about relationship. Kindred says you can prepare the meal together and figure it out as you go. Kindred leaves a few hours for the day or evening to unfold because real depth of relationship requires more than two hours' time.

It doesn't matter how big the table is or what it looks like. It doesn't really matter what kind of food is shared, as long as some care and intention goes into it. What matters is that the table is filled with heart and set with soul. I promise if you carve out a few hours for a slow meal and remove distractions (no cell phones!), something magical will happen. People will open up. People will connect. You—and everyone around that table—will start to uncover a little bit more of the Kindred Life.

WHOM TO GATHER WITH

The first obvious choice is close friends you already have. Very few people in Western culture, even in close friendships, take the time to spend long amounts of time together,

lingering around the table. Yet in so many other world cultures, this is the norm. Honestly, all you need is one other person to begin. If you don't have a single person who comes to mind, it's time to find someone. If you don't have someone to share your table with, you can be the first one to open the door.

The next choice is to invite people into the fold who don't have anyone. Maybe someone who is single or divorced or going through a hard time in their marriage. If you've ever been in one of these situations, you know how life changing it is to be welcomed into a sacred space of connection where you are seen.

WHAT TO EAT OR MAKE

A few options to get you started:

1. Choose some of the recipes in this book. The recipes I've included aren't fancy or meant to be impressive. But they do require effort and time because these things communicate that the people around you matter, and preparing a place for someone is a gift you can give them. The recipes in this book are a few steps above "get pizza delivered and throw it on the table with some paper plates" and several steps below "entertaining on your wedding china." Somewhere in the middle, there is a place for un-fancy yet intentional meals prepared with care for and even *with* the people who will be sharing the food around our imperfect tables.

2. Do you have a greatest dish—perhaps a family recipe or something you've made for years? Your grandma's tomato sauce? Your aunt's tamales? Your grandmother's fried rice? Choose one or two things that make you feel like "home" and are always foolproof—and make that.

3. Go to BonAppetit.com and pick something.

4. Have everyone bring a beverage to contribute: a bottle of wine, sparkling water, craft beer, or the makings of a great cocktail.

And then prepare the meal with your people. If you really want to make the entire meal by yourself, let the people you're gathering with do something to feel included and invested. *Remember, this isn't a performance.* People don't want to be entertained. They want a safe place where they belong. They want connection and to feel seen and known.

HOW TO CREATE SPACE

I know this might sound like a lot, but set aside four hours for this gathering. You might have to give something up that's sucking your time, but this matters, and it's worth it. This is about creating space for people to just *be* and savor the moment without rushing. If you can cover up the clocks so there's not a concept of time at all, even better! You *can* do this wherever you are, as long as you're focused on connection rather than perfection.

Make it clear that you want people around for a while—you're not just gonna eat and then send them home. This might feel foreign to some people at first, because we're all so used to busyness and timelines.

More ideas

- No phones at the table (get a phone basket).
- No TVs in the background.
- Kids on laps welcomed! Resist the urge to entertain or micromanage the kids. They, too, can be involved in helping make the food or prepare the space. If not, send them outside. It's amazing the games and imaginary play kids—from toddlers to teenagers—can come up with together when distractions and screens are removed.
- No shame at all, though, in putting on a movie for the kids so the adults can have enough time to connect. When we do this, we usually reserve it for later in the evening after the kids have already been involved in what we're doing and had some play time.

Fun flourishes

- Make napkins by cutting squares of mismatched fabric and leaving the edges raw.
- Use mason jars or upcycled jars to put flowers, branches, or greenery on the table.
- Decorate with candles. Always candles.
- Create a chill dinner playlist that you use every time. The songs will become your soundtrack.

Acknowledgments

Much love and thanks to . . .

My mom, Dawn: You gave me the gift of writing, a heart for adventure and wonder, and a foundation of faith in Jesus. You first showed me the importance of noticing splashes of beauty, starting with the crocuses outside my kindergarten classroom window. Thank you, Mom, for always pulling us over on the side of the road to marvel at a breathtaking landscape and for—literally—taking time to stop and smell the roses. I know your prayers carry me every day, everywhere I go. My dad, Frank: You showed me the value of hard work and always held out a strong, weathered hand to me whenever I needed it—as I learned to walk, as I stood in the waves on the Jersey shore, and as you steadied me down a hill on my wedding day. You've always been my cheerleader. Thank you for saying, "I've *always* known it," when I told you I was finally going to be a published writer! I hope this makes you proud. I can't thank you and Mom enough for giving me roots and also letting me fly.

My big brother, Glen: Thank you for watching over me when I was little, even the times I was too young to remember. Thanks for always saying yes when I wanted to come in your room and look at your yearbooks and Star Wars figurines and for not being too cool for your little sister whenever I came to visit you. I know you'll always be there for me. My sister-in-law, Trish: Thanks for being like my actual sister since I met you at age fourteen, for letting me borrow your clothes and makeup, and for always having a listening ear that pointed me to truth. Thank you for first giving me the role of Aunt Stine. You and Glen are both woven in this story as you've been a grounding place full of love, stability, and fun memories.

My parents-in-law, Ted and Kum: You have both worked so hard for so many years, and the fruits of that labor are a generous blessing to our family and will surely leave a legacy. What you have given and sacrificed will affect generations, and Steven and I cannot thank you enough. Thank you, also, for raising your little boy into a man who is strong, brave, hardworking, and the best cook I know—second to his mama, of course!

My sister-in-law, Michelle, and my brother-in-law, Cody: Even though I always wish we lived closer, I'm so grateful for all the memories we have throughout the years—cooking and eating epic meals, letting the cousins play for days on end, adventuring, and having great conversations. "It's all about the memories," indeed!

The beloved matriarch of the Bailey family, Jewell "Gran" Bailey: Thank you for your legacy of faith. The rest of the North Carolina family: I'm so grateful our children have so many memories with you and that your family traditions are now woven into my own.

Paula and Steve and the rest of my New Jersey family: Thank you for the laughter, your generosity and love, and for some of my earliest, most formative memories. Thank you especially to Aunt Lucille: Your table was always a fun, comforting place for me growing up. You'll always be with me in my kitchen and around my table.

My "heirloom friends" (a phrase Shannon coined): You are the ones who have been there through so many different life stages, seen me at my best and worst, and are like family now. You welcomed Steven without hesitation. You've cheered us on in this big kindred dream. You've encouraged me through the doubts and fears and reminded me of God's goodness and faithfulness on this journey, time and time again. If you're one of these friends, you know who you are, and you know how much I dearly love you.

Our "kindred friends": You are the ones who gather here at the farm regularly, stopping over to borrow a gardening tool, have a glass of wine at golden hour, or let the kids play for hours in the Forest of Fun. You share the beauty and messiness of daily life with us around the campfire and around the table. You know our family in an everyday way, and we know yours, and this is the meaning of true community. If you're one of these friends, you know who you are. Steven and I love you and couldn't do daily life without you.

My wise and kind agent, Jenni Burke, at Illuminate Literary: Thank you for pointing me to truth, for your belief in me as a writer, and for your diligence in finding the right publishing home for me. One day, we will drink wine in Italy together!

The incredible team at Harper Horizon: You have made a childhood dream of mine come true by publishing this book. Andrea Fleck-Nisbet: Thank you for your belief in this story— from the beginning, I knew we were speaking the same language. Amanda Bauch: Thank you for your encouraging words and for cheering me on to reach the finish line. Meaghan Porter: Thank you for walking me through the process of honing every single page of the book to make it beautiful and inspiring. Whitney Bak: Thank you for your work editing the manuscript so it could be the best possible offering. John Andrade: Thank you for your mad marketing skills to bring the message of this story to as many people as possible.

The Kindred Farm team, especially Tyson Ford and Grace Masters: You could just do an ordinary job, but you do it excellently, creating and serving with heart. I'm so thankful to have you on this team that feels like family.

The Kindred Farm Store customers and regulars: Thanks for driving the Tennessee backroads on Saturday mornings and sharing a bit of your lives with us. Our Kindred Dinners guests: Thanks for your vulnerability to show up around the table. You have all taught me so much about cultivating a life of connection, and I hope you always feel welcome on our land and around our tables.

Tsh Oxenreider: Thank you for welcoming me to the Art of Simple team and for making space for my voice on your blog and podcast, an opportunity that was the catalyst to writing this book.

Kirby Trapolino: When I met you and was invited into the Grassroots family, my life took a pivot that has led me all the way to today. Thank you for all the Frappuccinos, for giving me my first Mac computer (Tangerine Dream!), and most importantly, for your friendship and trust.

Barrett Ward: To this day, I'm so grateful for that phone call where you said, "So I have this idea . . ." and that you invited me to be a part of it. I'm so proud of the work we did together, and we had fun doing it! Thank you for friendship, for modeling bold leadership, and for encouraging me to grow.

Jeremy Cowart: Thank you for so many years of hilariousness and friendship with you and Shannon, and especially for your willingness to be a part of this project with your stunning photography. It means so much that you've been there since the beginning.

Sarah Gilliam: Thank you for your kindred spirit–ness, food styling fun, and desire to not just take photos but to tell stories through your photography. I'm so glad you've been a part of the real-life Kindred Dinners and this project.

Our Dallas friends: Your love and laughter have left imprints in my life forever; we had babies together, walked the neighborhood, and shared so many meals in eleven years. Special shout-out to our "PEFO" friends for all the plates of Yummy Cookies and the late nights playing Cranium on the maroon carpet in our condo in front of those super swank floor-to-ceiling mirrors.

Everyone involved with Urban Acres, from the very fledgling foundations to the end: Thank you for the ways you shared your lives with us and the community—growing food to share, working the register, sorting produce, hosting farm stands, taking care of animals, stocking shelves, and so much more. I'm changed by my relationships with you, and you each did something to make a difference in the way people are nourished in Dallas–Ft. Worth.

To my dear readers since the early days of DreamMore.com: You all believed in my writing and kept encouraging me to write a book one day. I hope holding this book in your hands makes you smile.

Doc and Stacy: There aren't words to adequately express the impact your guidance and wisdom have made on me, Steven, and generations to come. Thank you each for being with us during our darkest times, for guiding us down the path of hope, for showing us that the truth always, *always* sets you free. If not for you, this story would have unfolded very differently. Because of you, there is community. There is a future. And there is joy.

My precious girls, Luci and Norah: Thank you for being beautiful, wonderful you. Being a mama is the one thing I always wanted to be, and it's the absolute greatest gift to be yours! You inspire me every day with your wisdom, creativity, and kindness. Here's to all the fairy villages, flower bouquets, exploring waterfalls, nights sitting by the fire, joy rides in the Green Turtle, yummy meals cooked together, and bedtime stories under the twinkle lights that our hearts can hold. Shine on, girls. God is writing a beautiful story through each of you, and I can't wait to see it unfold as you grow!

The love of my life, Steven: Goodness, babe, what a journey. You've inspired me from day one with your adventurous heart, your transformative story of grace, the way you squeeze every drop out of life, and your intentional love that is unlike anything else I've known. I can't believe I get to be the one by your side. Thank you for believing in me before I believed in myself. Thank you for not allowing me to shrink back from this opportunity. Thank you for being an incredible husband and daddy and for always encouraging our family to do the brave, beautiful thing. Life with you is just the best.

♥

Christine

Notes

Chapter 1: Sing Your Song

1. William Jordan, "Why the Mockingbird Sings: And Why at Night, When Most Birds Sleep?," *Los Angeles Times*, January 25, 1987, https://www.latimes.com/archives/la-xpm -1987-01-25-tm-5613-story.html.

Chapter 7: It's Pronounced "Santa Fee"

1. Exodus 13:21.

Chapter 9: Learning to Ask for Help

1. Barbara Brown Taylor, *An Altar in the World* (London: Canterbury Press Norwich, 2009), 96.
2. Anne Lamott, *Traveling Mercies: Some Thoughts on Faith* (New York: Pantheon Books, 1999; repr. New York: Anchor Books, 2000), 82.

Chapter 10: You're Not Gonna Break

1. Robert Frost, "A Servant to Servants," in *North of Boston*, 2nd ed. (1915; repr. New York: Henry Holt and Company, 1917), 66, https://www.google.com/books/edition/North _of_Boston/A6QqAAAAMAAJ.
2. Urban Dictionary, s.v. "scrappy," no. 3, June 19, 2008, https://www.urbandictionary.com /define.php?term=scrappy.
3. 2 Corinthians 4:7–9 TPT.

Chapter 14: The Table Is for Everyone

1. Isaiah 25:6–8.

About the Author

Christine Marie Bailey is a grateful farmer, writer, and dreamer. A former music industry gal turned social entrepreneur turned sustainable produce and flower farmer, Christine is growing deep roots with her chef husband, Steven, on their seventeen-acre Kindred Farm in Santa Fe, Tennessee. She's passionate about homeschooling her two wild and free daughters and will always say yes to waterfall chasing, campfire sitting, and eating ice cream on the roof under a country sky. She shares adventures and inspiration on her website, ChristineMarieBailey.com.